John Horace McFarland

Floral Designs, Series I

a hand-book for cut-flower workers and florists

John Horace McFarland

Floral Designs, Series I
a hand-book for cut-flower workers and florists

ISBN/EAN: 9783337272456

Printed in Europe, USA, Canada, Australia, Japan

Cover: Foto ©Andreas Hilbeck / pixelio.de

More available books at **www.hansebooks.com**

FLORAL DESIGNS

SERIES I

A Hand-Book for Cut-Flower Workers and Florists

COMPILED BY

J. HORACE McFARLAND

INCLUDING

PRACTICAL HINTS ON FLORAL WORK

BY

MRS. ELLA GRANT CAMPBELL

PUBLISHED BY

A. BLANC AND J. HORACE McFARLAND

1888

▲   — -

ENGRAVINGS

By A. Blanc, Engraver for Florists, Seedsmen
and Nurserymen, Philadelphia, Pa.

PRINTING

By J. Horace McFarland, Printer for Nurserymen,
Florists and Seedsmen, Harrisburg, Pa.

PREFACE.

THIS LITTLE BOOK, upon which unusual labor has been expended, is offered to the cut-flower workers and florists of the country with the sincere hope that they will find it useful to them in their everyday work. It is an experiment; yet the publishers feel assured that it will be a successful one, because such a work has long been needed. Substitutes, in the shape of collections of photographs, are to be met with occasionally, only making more apparent the general need of some means for showing how floral designs look when actually made up, as well as of offering suggestions to the florist and his customers.

In selecting designs for illustrations, great care has been taken to present only those of moderate cost and difficulty, such as will be constantly useful to the large majority of florists. Many superior effects have been regretfully laid aside because of their too elaborate character or too great cost, rendering them seldom or never available to many florists. The publishers hope to present in a future volume a set of larger designs, should the present work be found generally acceptable.

The complete analysis of these designs, and the elaborate treatise on the proper handling of floral work and decorations (beginning page 105), will be found useful and suggestive, as showing how these things are done by a thoroughly successful artist. And the many suggestions of designs and effects suitable for all occasions will doubtless save much thought and worry if frequently referred to.

To those friends who have assisted, in suggestions and in furnishing designs, as well as to those who have encouraged us by advance subscriptions, are due the hearty thanks of

THE PUBLISHERS.

ℰONTENTS.

CONTRIBUTORS OF DESIGNS.

The thanks of the publishers are due to the floral artists who have so kindly assisted us by supplying designs for engraving. Their names are noted below, together with the numbers of the designs contributed by each.

W. E. Bowditch, Boston 12
A. Blanc, Philadelphia 20, 31, 32, 37, 42, 43
Mrs. Ella Grant Campbell, Cleveland . 3, 4, 5, 6, 7, 8, 10, 11, 13, 19, 21, 45, 46
J. D. Carmody, Evansville, Indiana 1, 18, 16, 17
N. L. Chrestensen, Erfurt (Germany) . . . 34, 47, 48, 49, 50
B. A. Elliott & Co., Pittsburgh, Pa 33, 35, 38
Hugh Graham & Sons, Philadelphia 14
C. H. Grigg, Philadelphia 2, 9, 15, 20, 21, 23, 25, 26, 28, 30
Robert J. Halliday, Baltimore, Md. 36
Joseph Kift, Baltimore, Md. 44, 46
Daniel B. Long, Buffalo 39, 40, 41
Philadelphia Floral Co. 27
R. E. Shufhelt, Chatham, N. Y. 22

FLORAL DESIGNS

NO. 1. STANDING CROSS.

Size, _____   Price, _____

Size, __   Price, _____

Size, __ __   __   Price, _

NO. 1. STANDING CROSS AND PILLOW.

NO. 2. STANDING CROSS OF IVY.

Size.   Price.

Size,   Price,

Size,   Price,

NO 2. STANDING CROSS OF IVY.

Size.   Price.

Size.   Price.

Size.   Price,

NO. 3. CROSS WITH SLANTING ARMS.

Size,   Price,

Size,   Price,

Size,   Price,

NO. 4. IMMORTELLE CROSS.

NO. 5. WREATH.

Size, _____ _____   Price, _____

Size, _   Price, _____ _

Size,   ___ ___ _   Price, ___ _

NO. 6. WREATH.

Size,   Price,

Size,   Price,

Size,   Price,

NO. 6. WREATH, WITH LARGE BOW OF RIBBON.

Size,   Price,

Size,   Price,

Size,   Price,

Size,   Price,

Size,   Price,

Size,   Price,

NO. 8. MASONIC WREATH.

NO. 9. SICKLE AND SHEAF.

Size,   Price,

Size,   Price,

Size,   Price,

NO. 9. SICKLE AND SHEAF.

NO. 10. FLAT SICKLE.

Size.   Price.

Size,   Price,

Size,   Price,

NO. 11. PILLOW.

Size,   Price,

Size,   Price,

Size,   Price,

NO. 12. STANDING ANCHOR.

Size,   Price,

Size,   Price,

Size,   Price,

ENGRAVING
COPYRIGHTED
BY A.BLANC.

NO. 13. BROKEN COLUMN.

Size,   Price,

Size,   Price,

Size.   Price,

NO. 13. BROKEN COLUMN.

NO. 14. FLORAL SCROLL.

Size,   Price,

Size,   Price,

Size,   Price.

NO. 14. FLORAL SCROLL, WITH CROSS AND CROWN.

NO. 15. HARP ON BASE.

Size,   Price,

Size,   Price,

Size.   Price.

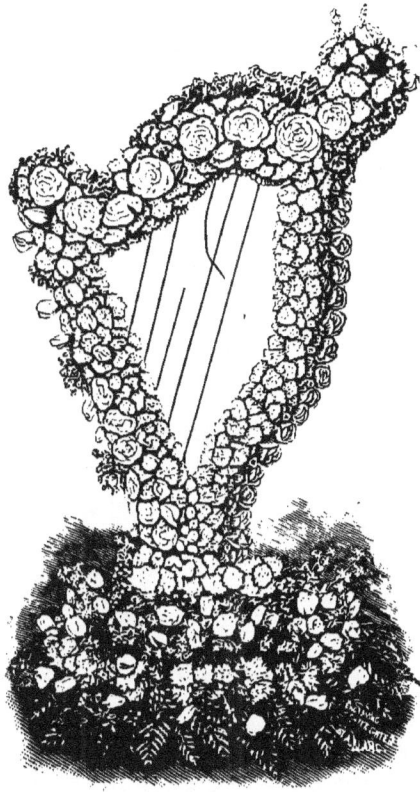

NO. 16. TRUE HARP.

Size.   Price,

Size,   Price,

Size,   Price,

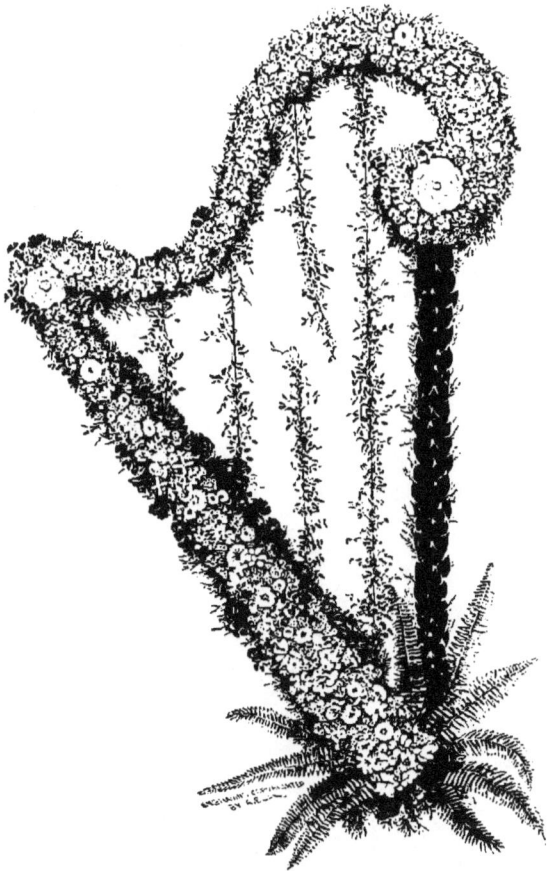

NO. 16. TRUE HARP.

NO. 17. LYRE ON BASE.

Size,   _ .   Price,

Size,   . _   . _ . .   Price,   _

Size,   Price,

NO. 17. LYRE ON BASE.

Size.   Price,

Size,   Price,

Size.   Price.

NO. 18. CROSS, PILLOW AND ARCH.

NO. 19. BROKEN WHEEL.

Size,   Price,

Size,   Price,

Size,   Price,

NO. 19. BROKEN WHEEL ON IVY BASE.

NO. 20. BANNER, WITH CROSS.

Size,   _ ..   Price,

Size,..   Price,

Size,   Price,

NO. 20. BANNER, WITH CROSS.

NO. 21. ARM CHAIR.

Size,   Price,

Size,   Price,

Size,_____   Price,

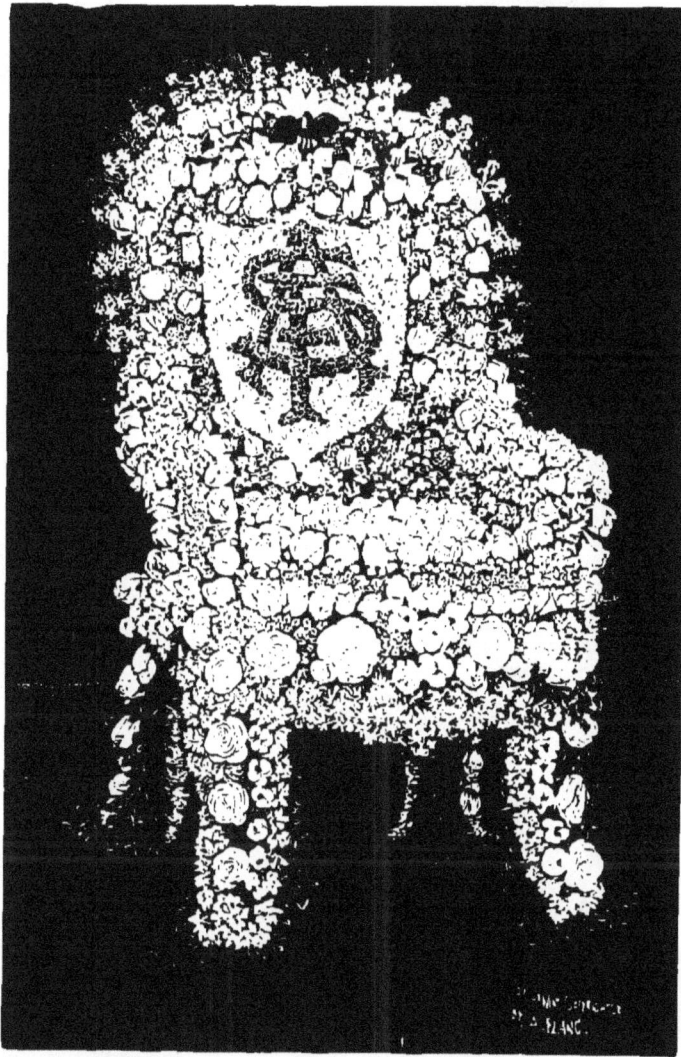

NO. 21. ARM CHAIR, WITH MONOGRAM.

NO. 22. FRAMED PANEL

Size. _ Price.

Size. Price.

Size, Price, _

NO. 22. FRAMED PANEL.

NO. 23. WATER LILY BASKET.

Size, _____ _____ _____ Price, _____ ____

Size, _____ _____ Price, _____ _____ _____

Size, _____ Price, _____

FIGURE 23

NO. 23. WATER LILY AND FERN BASKET

NO. 24. ROSE BASKET.

Size,   Price,

Size.   Price,

Size,   —   Price,

NO. 24. ROSE BASKET.

NO. 25. HAMPER OF ROSES.

Size,   Price,

Size,   Price,

Size,   Price,

NO. 25. BASKET OF ROSES.

NO. 26. CHAMPAGNE BASKET.

Size,   Price,

Size,   Price,

Size,   Price,

NO. 26. CHAMPAGNE BASKET.

NO. 27. GATES AJAR, WITH STAR.

Size, _____   Price,___

Size,   Price, _____

Size,   Price, _____

NO. 27. GATES AJAR. WITH STAR

NO. 28. GATES AJAR.

Size,......................... Price, . ___

Size,___ . . . Price.

Size, _ Price, ___

NO. 28. GATES AJAR.

NO. 29. WREATH, WITH PALM LEAVES.

Size,_____ _ _ _____   Price,_____

Size,   . .   Price, ... _

Size,   Price,_ _ _ _ _

NO. 29. WREATH WITH PALM LEAVES.

NO. 30. FLORAL VASE OR URN

Size,   Price,

Size,   Price,

Size,   Price,

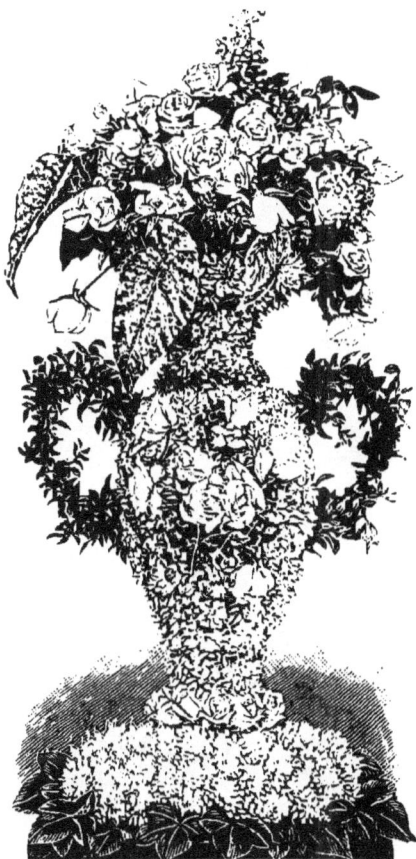

NO. 30. FLORAL VASE OR URN.

NO. 31. CRESCENT.

Size.   Price,

Size.   Price,

Size,   Price,

NO. 32. FLORAL HORSESHOE.

Size.   Price,

Size.   Price,

Size,   Price,

NO. 32. FLORAL HORSESHOE.

NO. 33. FAN ON EASEL.

Size,   Price,

Size,   Price,

Size,   Price,

ENGRAVED
COPYRIGHTED BY. A. BLANC.

NO. 34. STANDING FAN.

Size, _____ Price, __

Size, Price,

Size, __ _ ___ Price, __ _ ___

NO. 34. STANDING FAN.

NO. 35. VASE OR FONT.

Size,   Price,

Size.   Price,

Size,   Price,

NO. 36. FLORAL PIANO.

Size, ____   Price, ____

Size,   Price, ____

Size, ____   Price,

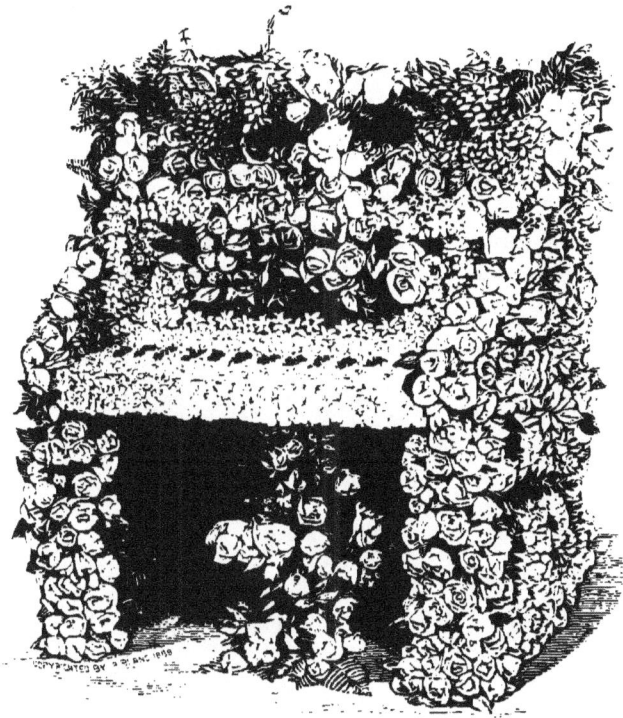

NO. 37. HORN OF PLENTY.

Size,   Price,

Size,   Price,

Size,   Price,

NO. 38. MIRROR DECORATION

Size,   Price,

Size,   Price,

Size,   Price,

NO. 38. MIRROR DECORATION.

NO. 39. BRIDE'S HAND BOUQUET.

Size,   Price,_____

Size,   Price,

Size,   Price,

ENGRAVING COPYRIGHTED
BY A.BLANC.

NO. 40. CUPID'S YOKE.

Size,   Price,

Size,   _   Price,

Size,   Price,

NO. 40. CUPID'S YOKE.

NO. 41. LOVERS' KNOT.

Size, _____   _____   Price, _____

Size, ___   __   _ __   Price, ___ __

Size, ___   __ ____   Price, __ _ __

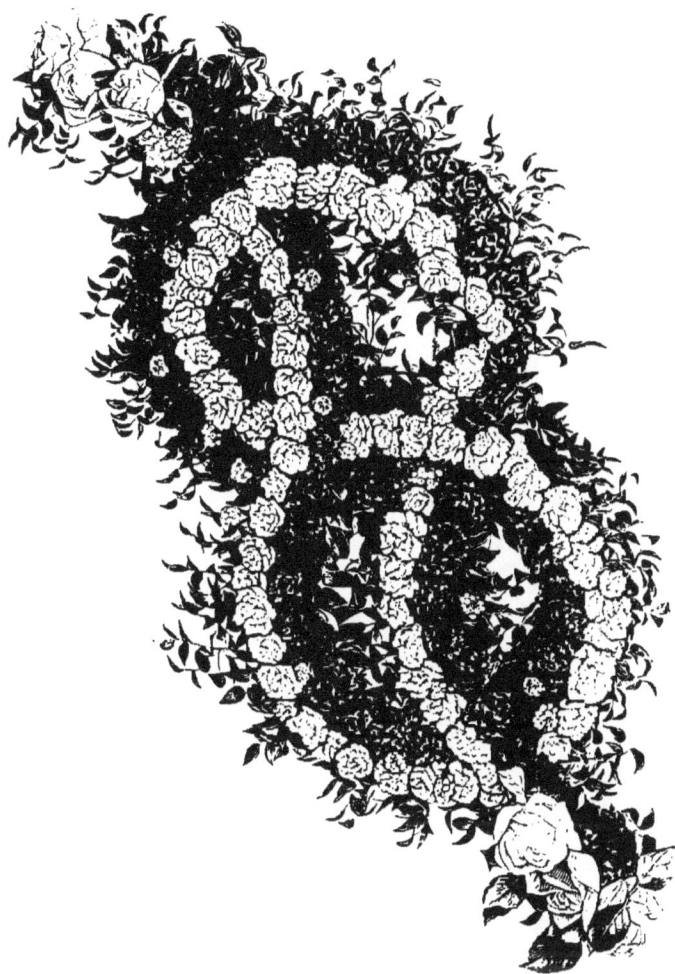

NO. 42. CUPID'S BOW.

Size,   Price,

Size, ___.   Price,

Size, .   Price,

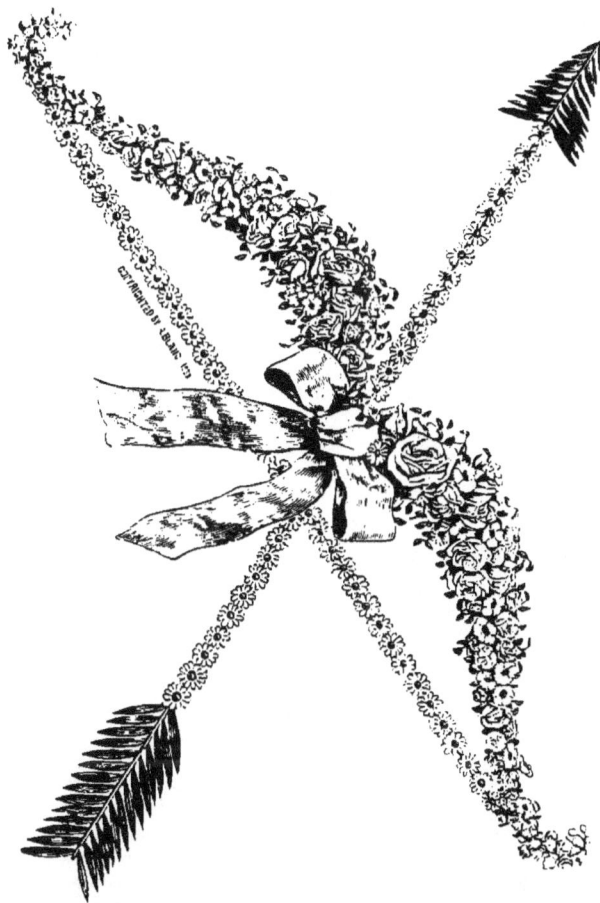

NO. 42. CUPID'S BOW.

NO. 43. SHOE. FILLED WITH ROSES.

Size,   Price,

Size,   Price,

Size,   Price,

NO. 43. SHOE, FILLED WITH ROSES.

NO. 44. SHEATH OF BIRCH BARK.

Size,   Price,

NO. 45. BROKEN HOPES.

Size,   Price,

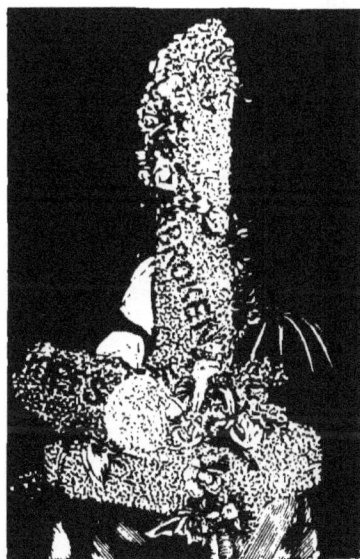

NO. 44. SHEATH OF BIRCH BARK.
NO. 45. BROKEN HOPES.

NO. 46. BASKET ON PANEL.

Size.   Price,

NO. 47. LILY BUD BASKET.

Size,   Price,

NO. 46. BASKET ON PANEL.
NO. 47. LILY BUD BASKET.

NO. 48. CAMP KETTLE.

Size,   Price,

Size,   Price,

Size,   Price,

NO. 48. CAMP KETTLE.

NO. 49. GERMAN DESIGN.

Size, _ _ _ _ _ _ _ _ _ _ _ _ _ _ Price, _

Size, _ _ _ _ _ _ _ _ _ _ _ _ _ _ Price, _

Size, _ _ _ _ _ _ _ _ _ _ _ _ _ _ Price,

NO. 49. GERMAN DESIGN OF GRASSES, ETC.

NO. 50. WINTER BOUQUET.

Size,   Price,

Size,   Price,

Size,   Price,

NO. 50. WINTER BOUQUET OF GRASSES. ETC.

ANALYSIS OF DESIGNS.

Analysis of Designs Illustrated.

—

IN CRITICISING the designs presented in the foregoing pages, it should be kept in mind that they are largely intended to be only *suggestive*, as showing about how certain forms of designs look when filled. They are not presented as models to follow exactly, but mainly for the purpose of aiding sales in the flower-store or greenhouse office ; and the customer's taste can ofttimes be as well suited, or better, by a wide departure from the forms here presented. Indeed, the different seasons will frequently make necessary the use of other flowers than those indicated in the plates.

Again, it is hoped that the use of this book will stimulate originality in the working florists who seek its aid. In the successive seasons of the year very many different forms of the same idea can be developed, and we trust, that with the many suggestions as to other useful designs for various occasions presented in the following pages, our brother florists may find their inventive ideas stimulated to the point of producing many designs of greater beauty than any here shown or described.

No. 1. (Page 9.) **Standing Cross and Pillow.** As the engraver very plainly indicates, the flowers used are candidum lilies, roses, callas, abutilons, carnations, sweet alyssum, drooping begonias and a few dainty pansies. It represents a medium-priced design, with smilax backing. See page 133 for other combinations.

No. 2. (Page 11.) **Standing Cross of Ivy.** A standing ivy cross, intermingled with Perle roses. Vinca elegantissima is climbing around and over it, and heads of wheat are arranged in the base as per illustration. For descriptions of other ivy designs, see page 136.

No. 3. (Page 13.) **Cross with Slanting Arms.** This design was made up in the summer, and was about three feet high with the base. The engraving clearly indicates the character of the flowers used, but does not do justice to the real beauty of the design. For descriptions other crosses, see pages 134, 135 and 136.

No. 4. (Page 15.) **Immortelle Cross.** A square standing cross of rich purple immortelles, with drapery of Marie Guillot roses. A bunch of marguerites were grouped as though growing; fern leaves, lily of the valley, etc., were disposed in a careless fashion on the base. The reverse of this cross was filled with polished ivy leaves, with a base of white immortelles, representing a rock. On the rock was the one word " Faith." The idea sought to be embodied was " Friendship and Immortality," represented by ivy and immortelles. The design is suitable for the funeral of an aged lady.

No. 5. (Page 17.) **Wreath.** A pretty and inexpensive wreath of mixed flowers, tied with No. 16 white satin ribbon. It consists of Perle and Marechal Niel roses, carnations, primroses and lily of the valley. Smilax and ferns were used for backing. Very effective for its cost.

No. 6. (Page 19.) **Wreath, with Large Bow of Ribbon.** This is a more expensive wreath, and is one form of the much admired crescent wreath. It can be made either on a stand or flat. A solid wreath of white carnations without the admixture of any other flower forms the ground-work of the design. Pale Mermet roses and their foliage are arranged loosely on this ground-work of carnations, narrowing down to a single bud. The whole is in strong relief against the white below it. Lily of the valley clusters to the left of the ribbon sash, which in this case is pearl white satin, No. 20; 2½ yards were used in the sash. For further details, see article on making up a wreath, in Chapter I, page 119.

No. 7. (Page 21.) **Standing Wreath, on Base.** Niphetos roses and carnations, interspersed with lily of the valley, heavily backed with smilax, are the main features of this work. It is a representative piece as turned out of many floral establishments.

No. 8. (Page 23.) **Masonic Wreath, enclosing Square and Compass.** An admixture of flowers enter into this design, which are plainly indicated in the engraving. For descriptions of other wreaths, see Chapter V, page 132.

No. 9. (Page 25.) **Sickle and Sheaf.** Sickle of Niphetos roses, carnations, bouvardias and lily of the valley. The handle was of blue Roman hyacinths, laid against a standing sheaf of wheat.

No. 10. (Page 27.) **Flat Sickle.** This is a low-priced design, and is made of the same flowers as the preceding one. The wheat is here arranged as though it had just been cut by the sickle and had fallen over the blade. For other designs of sickles, see chapter on funeral work, page 132.

No. 11. (Page 29.) **Pillow.** This was arranged in the month of September, when there is a dearth of good flowers. A delicately-tinted pink dahlia occupies the four corners of the pillow, while a crescent arrangement is shown on the pillow, which contains the sacred word "Mother." The foundation of the lettering is of white carnations. For further descriptions of pillows, see chapter on funeral work, page 133.

No. 12. (Page 31.) **Standing Anchor.** A pretty low-priced design, such as is called for every day. In a small anchor there is always difficulty in obtaining distinctness of outline. Observe carefully our directions for packing the corners of such designs, on page 119.

No. 12. (Page 33.) **Broken Column.** The shaft is of white carnations, interspersed with roses, lilies, tuberoses, etc. It is an ordinary every-day column. Another arrangement is seen on page 95, lettered with "Broken Hopes." For descriptions of other columns, see chapter on funeral designs, page 133.

No. 14. (Page 35.) **Floral Scroll, with Cross and Crown.** Polished ivy leaves are the foundation of this work. Perle roses outline the edge, while a row of marguerites add a finishing touch. "Rest" is lettered on white cape flowers, while the Cross and Crown is formed of roses. The back is covered with smilax. A rich piece of work, and very effective.

No. 15. (Page 37.) **Harp on Base.** This is the usual form of a harp. It is formed almost entirely of roses, camellias and chrysanthemums. The strings are made of silver wire, with one of them broken as in engraving. Roman hyacinths are interspersed among the flowers on the base, which is finished with a heavy border of fern leaves.

No. 16. (Page 39.) **True Harp.** This is a simple but beautiful piece, made of all small flowers, with the exception of two camellias which form rosettes. White jasmine, bouvardias, primroses and sweet alyssum form the frame, with laurel leaves overlapping, to supply the other upright side. Fern leaves finish the base, as seen in the engraving. The strings are covered with smilax, ; asparagus would also be well for this.

No. 17. (Page 41.) **Lyre on Base.** The engraving clearly delineates the character of this design. The flowers enumerated above are all represented in its composition. The back is covered with ground pine, or bouquet green. The base is finished with ivy leaves.

No. 18. (Page 43.) **Cross, Pillow and Arch.** This design is most appropriate for a Catholic funeral. A variety of flowers is used, as may be noted in the engraving. Lilies, abutilons, bouvardias and roses are the main constituents, and the piece is heavily backed by tradescantia leaves.

No. 19. (Page 45.) **Broken Wheel, on Ivy Base.** This beautiful wheel was made for a railroad magnate who had passed away. On an embankment of polished ivy leaves were rails of violets. The wheel itself stood thirty inches high. The outer edge or "tire" was formed of white camellias set closely together. The "felloe" and "hub" were of white carnations, while the "spokes" were of two rows of white azaleas. The "nut" was indicated by a white camellia. Ferns were grouped in graceful clumps at the rear of the wheel, while a mass of Roman hyacinths and marguerites "grew" on the bank to the left, intermingled with delicate ferns. The beauty of this design consisted of the pure white wheel, no tinted flowers being allowed in it, and the strong contrast afforded by the dark green ivy leaves on the base.

No. 20. (Page 47.) **Banner, with Cross.** This very simple and chaste design presents a banner of ivy leaves, on which is arranged a cross of lily of the valley with a single Niphetos bud in the center. Three callas are arranged, connected by ribbon as in the engraving. A floral base of marguerites, fern leaves and roses, completes this admirable arrangement. For further suggestions, see Chapter V.

No. 21. (Page 49.) **Armchair, with Monogram.** An armchair upholstered in roses, carnations, etc. An emblem of ease, and supposed to be very emblematic of the life a florist leads, which we all know is largely easy chairs and flowers! All play and no work —a charming life! Anyone desirous of filling such a chair can do so in the most approved fashion by consulting the arrangement so admirably engraved on page 49.

No. 22. (Page 51.) **Framed Panel.** A panel of lycopodium, or live green moss, framed in ivy leaves. A graceful cluster of callas and foliage, orchids and Roman hyacinths, tied with sash of ribbon, as the subject of the picture. A scarlet anthurium gives the only touch of color to this simple and beautiful tribute. Endless variations can be made on this suggestion by the artistic worker.

No. 23. (Page 53.) **Water Lily and Fern Basket.** A charming arrangement is here depicted, with touches of adiantum ferns. The long loose stems of the water lilies are very artistically managed. The engraving gives a good idea of the filling.

No. 24. (Page 55.) **Rose Basket.** A square gilt basket of Perle roses and fern leaves. A cluster of silvery white Rex begonia leaves occupies the center, with a few light blue pansies placed in relief against it, which gives the touch of beauty to the whole.

No. 25. (Page 57.) **Basket of Roses.** Perle and American Beauty roses are illustrated, with their own foliage. The only departure is the cluster of bouvardia in the center.

No. 26. (Page 59.) **Champagne Basket.** Mermet roses, lily of the valley and foliage; a cluster of orchids, with a clump of sunny-faced pansies. The left side of this basket was of Niphetos roses. For suggestions for other baskets, see Chapter II, page 125.

No. 27. (Page 61.) **Gates Ajar, with Star.** This design is a very popular one with a certain class of patrons, and is a beautiful design when well made. The engraving depicts a summer arrangement of this design. The arch supporting two doves is made of carnations, single tuberoses and single flowers of gladiolus; star of the same. The whole design is edged heavily with euphorbia marginata, ("Snow on the Mountain"), the base being finished with sprays of asparagus tenuissimus; spikes of light colored gladiolus and longiflorum lilies are arranged on the base as indicated on page 61.

No. 28. (Page 63.) **Gates Ajar.** Another arrangement of this design. An arch, surmounted by three lilies, probably representing the "Trinity." Lilium candidum, Niphetos roses, jasmine, carnations and bouvardias are the materials employed. For other arrangements, see chapter on funeral designs, page 134.

No. 29. (Page 65.) **Wreath, with Palm Leaves.** A beautiful wreath of lily of the valley, interspersed with roses. Two palm leaves (Cycas revoluta) are fastened, as in the engraving, with knot of white satin ribbon, which, with the addition of a calla, a eucharis and a few light pansies, completes this fine memorial wreath.

No. 30. (Page 67.) **Floral Vase or Urn.** This is sometimes used as a funeral offering, and in the present instance is so designed. The vase is formed of white carnations, with cluster of roses on the side; the handles are of smilax. Niphetos roses, with begonia leaves, form the filling of the vase. Easily varied for other than funeral occasions, and susceptible of artistic handling.

No. 31. (Page 69.) **Crescent.** Lilies, roses and marguerites, with undertoning of bouvardia; smilax and adiantum sprays finish the under edges.

No. 32. (Page 71.) **Floral Horseshoe.** A graceful arrangement of this popular emblem of "good luck." The ground-work is entirely of one variety of pansies. The main feature of this piece of work is the artistic arrangement of the lilium auratum and Perle roses, with the corresponding cluster of long-stemmed roses in relief, which completes this exquisite floral souvenir.

No. 33. (Page 73.) **Fan or Easel.** A lovely embellishment to any decoration is the fan here depicted. A feathery edge of lily of the valley, with a double row of marguerites forms the edge; rich purple pansies the body part, with "sticks" of white Roman hyacinths and spaces of white carnations, while ribbon finishes the handle. A few exquisite specimens of Perle roses, with sprays of adiantum foliage arranged as in cut, completes the fan, which in this case is resting on an easel of smilax.

No. 34. (Page 75.) **Standing Fan.** An exquisite piece of work is here illustrated. The artist has carried this design out in detail to a most elaborate finish. The spread of the fan is of rich crimson carnations, while the scolloped edge is formed of white flowers of the same. The fringing of lily of the valley is set so compactly together, that it resembles delicate lace or waving ostrich tips. The "sticks" were of bride's myrtle on ground of white, the handle being finished with cluster of buds, and a long loose knot of white ribbon. A rich decoration, consisting of cattleyas, roses and lilies, finished this superb piece of work.

No. 35. (Page 77.) **Vase or Font.** This is suitable either as a font, for christening purposes, or for Easter; or, it can be arranged as a vase. The first thing that commands our attention is the beautiful arrangement of the roses, and graceful position of the doves or sparrows. The edge of the font is massed heavily with lily of the valley. A narrow band of sweet alyssum is just beneath, while the under part of the bowl consists of white carnations. The pedestal is also formed of the same, with a line of Niphetos roses to form an edge. The standard consists of sweet alyssum. A drapery of Niphetos roses, with the sparrows as indicated in the engraving, finishes this chaste and beautiful design.

No. 36. (Page 79.) **Floral Piano.** This was made as a funeral design for the superintendent of a piano factory. It was richly "veneered" with Marechal Niel, Perle, Mermet, Niphetos and La France roses and adiantum ferns. The pedals were also composed of the same. The "key-board" was formed of white carnations and Marie Louise violets. The back and inside were of fern leaves and smilax. An elaborate piece of work, requiring high finish. The one illustrated stood four feet high.

No. 37. (Page 81.) **Horn of Plenty,** pouring forth a profusion of fruit and flowers, the whole being reflected in a square mirror edged with smilax. The horn can be made either of white or golden chrysanthemums, loaded with Perle and Bennett roses, intermingled with choice fruits and flowers as in illustration. Certainly a fine design for table use.

No. 38. (Page 83.) **Mirror Decoration.** This is part of a ball room decoration at Delmonico's. Laurel wreathing, with garlands of roses and carnations, backed with laurel, forms a "frieze" of flowers and foliage around the upper part of the room. A curtain drapery of asparagus tenuissimus is "caught up" to the top of the mirror, and brought to one side, falling in a careless profusion to the floor, concealing the pots of hybrid roses and clematis banked at the base of the mirror. The door-ways and windows were outlined with laurel wreathing, while garlands were suspended in each. Palms were scattered throughout the room and added much to the general effect.

No. 39. (Page 85.) **Bride's Hand Bouquet.** In the most perfect taste. The flowers used are readily perceived to be Bride roses and adiantum fronds. The article on hand bouquets has covered this ground completely. See page 129.

No. 40. (Page 87.) **Cupid's Yoke.** This was made with one-half of the design white and the other half pink roses and carnations, emblemizing "purity" and "love." The illustration gives the method employed in this case to reach this satisfactory result.

No. 41. (Page 89.) **Lovers' Knot.** Scarlet and white are employed to delineate clearly our subject of a true lover's knot. The ends are of rose buds, with smilax backing. This is a very effective wedding design.

No. 42. (Page 91.) **Cupid's Bow and Arrow.** This dainty affair is surely pretty enough to pierce any tender heart. The materials employed consist of roses and marguerites, edged with delicate sprigs of smilax, the ends of the bow being lily of the valley. The arrow is formed of a long cycas palm leaf, trimmed into proper shape, the shaft being covered with a single row of marguerites.

No. 43. (Page 93.) **Shoe, Filled with Roses.** This well-proportioned adjunct of feminine wear contains a more beautiful "filling" than falls to the lot of many of its kindred. The engraving so well individualizes the flowers employed that it is unnecessary to enumerate them. Appropriate as a gift, or for a wedding present.

No. 44. (Page 95.) **Sheath of Birch Bark.** Filled as in illustration. Marguerites and roses, tied with a ribbon. A pretty little souvenir gift.

No. 45. (Page 95.) **Broken Hopes.** "Broken Hopes" represent the feelings of the bereaved parents whose only son had through an accident been burned to death. The broken end of the shaft is laid on the base. A garland of roses winds around and conceals the shattered end. The whole design, shaft and base, is made of white carnations.

No. 46. (Page 97.) **Basket on Panel.** A very pretty subject is here illustrated, and one easy to work up. Suitable as part of house decoration, or as a souvenir gift. The panel is of velvet, and the basket made by cutting in half an ordinary oblong basket, or nicker "vase."

No. 47. (Page 97.) **Lily Bud Basket.** A wild rush-like arrangement of water lilies and swamp grass. The engraving gives a very good idea of the composition of this basket.

No. 48. (Page 99.) **Camp Kettle, filled with Flowers, Ferns and Grasses.** A very fine arrangement is here shown, formed of rare greenhouse flowers, choice fronds of ferns, and native and foreign grasses.

No. 49. (Page 101.) **German Design of Grasses, etc.** Illustrates the German idea of handling winter grasses, etc.

No. 50. (Page 103.) **Winter Bouquet of Grasses.** A gorgeous vase of dried grasses, peacock feathers, pampas plumes, etc. A sparrow has just alighted, and flutters on a spear of grass. Also a German design.

☞ *See page 149 for complete list of designs and arrangements suggested or described in addition to the above.*

Practical Hints
on Floral Work

PREFACE.

THE FOLLOWING pages are intended to supplement the idea of this work by giving, as expressed in the title, some practical hints as to floral work in its far-reaching modern development. The information here introduced is intended for the florist, not for the customer, for which reason it is "out of the way" of the actual designs themselves, yet convenient for reference at all times.

The directions may be more minute than many of the older and more experienced workers consider necessary; but it should be born in mind that very many who will use this work are far away from large cities, and though lacking in opportunity to see the work of others, are constantly called upon for a wide range of designs. To such the details may be welcome, and the variety that can be given to floral work from action upon these thoughts may prove to be helpful and profitable.

The aim of the author has been to present a large variety of ideas, with the hope that all may find some thought worth developing, or some suggestion that will fit their need. And that the florist who reads may reap a plentiful harvest of golden "shekels" though the growth of any ideas whose seed may have been gathered in these pages, is the dearest wish of

THE AUTHOR.

CHAPTER I.

.

THE MECHANICAL WORK.

HIS IS THE BEGINNER'S starting point—his first initiation into the florists' art. The rapidity and neatness with which he learns to do his work determines his chances of after success. The necessary materials to commence work with are : Pine tooth-picks, sharpened both ends ; match-sticks, six inches long ; annealed wire, Nos. 20, 22 and 36 ; unbleached linen thread of from No. 8 to 20, and a pair of heavy shears to cut wire with.

TO STEM A FLOWER.

There are two methods in use. One is : Cut the fine wire (No. 36) into lengths of about four inches ; wrap the wire around the tooth-pick, holding it firm ; place the flower in position, with the tooth-pick well up under the calyx, and with a few more quick wraps of the wire it is firmly secured. Tooth-picks by this process can be got ready before it is necessary to use them, thus saving time when in a hurry. The objection to this system is, that sometimes too much or not enough wire will be used to securely fasten the flower without slipping. The method I prefer is as follows : Separate the fine wire into small coils ; cut through these once, leaving the wire as one long length ; wrap a strand around it so as to prevent tangling. Place a coil of this fine wire around the neck, cut the tooth-picks to a proper length—whole, halves, or three-quarters, as the case may be—and you are ready for work. To wire for compact work, place the tooth-pick close up under the flower ; give three or four quick wraps of the wire around the two, *running the wire below the stem or calyx down onto the tooth-pick proper.* This is an important point, and prevents slipping. To break the wire : .Throw a loop over the end of the first finger of the right hand, slip this loop off between the firmly-held thumb and finger of the left hand, give the wire held in the right hand a quick pull, and the wire ties itself into a "kink" between the thumb and finger, breaking easily. Roll the short end left between the thumb and finger and the operation is complete. This can be done very rapidly by a good "wirer," and takes but a fraction of the time necessary to describe it.

Flowers for designs or baskets are divided into two general classes ; "body" and "surface" flowers. Body flowers are stemmed with the pick attached close under the blossom, while surface flowers are allowed a length of stem necessary for the position they are to occupy. This depends on the design and the individual taste of the worker.

TO WIRE A FLOWER.

To wire roses, carnations and other long-stemmed flowers, use No. 22 wire, cut into suitable length for the purpose required. Pierce the calyx of the rose or carnation, turning the end of the wire over but slightly ; give one or two twists of the wire around the stem, taking care to bring at the same time all the green leaves into proper place. Do not wrap the wire around too many times. This is a common mistake, and should be avoided. If the flowers are to be used for baskets, on the bases of designs, or other places where long-stemmed flowers are required, it will be necessary, after running the wire down the stem, to fasten a tooth-pick or match-stick onto it : do this with the same wire you used for running down the stem. For light roses, such as Bon Silene, Safrano, and roses of that weight, use No. 22 wire. American Beauty, La France, large Mermet, The Bride and all hybrid roses require No. 20 or 21 wire to support them properly.

No floral work will be light or graceful if too heavy wires are used, while too light wire will not retain the desired position of the flower. Iron annealed is better than the "bright" wire, so-called, as the latter has a spring in it, which causes it to get out of place. The same grade and number of wire may be "soft" or "hard." The "soft" grades will be found to be the most pliable and useful. Long-stemmed carnations are best on No. 22. Heavy hybrid roses require match-sticks to support their weight properly, when arranged in loose work. The skillful wirer will *always* study to bring the foliage so into shape by the wire that it will enhance the beauty of the flower.

MOSSING, TINFOILING, ETC.

For mossing floral designs nothing has yet superseded sphagnum. It is used universally. It seems to be the lightest, it retains the moisture the longest, and is the cleanest and most convenient material we have to handle. Where wood moss is plentiful, and can be had of a bright green color, a lining of it, with the balance of space filled in with sphagnum, is desirable. Where green moss cannot be obtained, tinfoil is the next best substitute.

Having pressed the water out of your sphagnum with a package of tinfoil, and with a spool of unbleached thread lying before you, you can commence mossing.

Having a wire form, for instance, a wreath, before you, take a sheet of tinfoil; lap over half an inch running around the wreath, press the tinfoil smoothly into the inside of the wreath; trim off all surplus over half an inch; fold over inside edge, and it is finished.

Some designs are tinfoiled on the outside, and others on the inside— the way the forms are made must determine this point. Now put in your moist sphagnum, filling *from bottom to top* as you go along. Remember, good work *cannot* be made on a poor, shaky foundation. *Firm packing, evenly distributed, thoroughly tied in with strong linen thread* (string is slovenly), *is the very ground-work of success.*

Be careful about packing corners in stars, crosses, and in all sharp angles; have all of these well filled out. Standing designs, if not well packed, will fall to pieces when they are moved, and your best efforts be ruined. "Tying-in" is the next thing on the programme. This should be done by holding the design and drawing the thread as tightly as it will allow without breaking, pressing down with the thumbs the sphagnum into place as you proceed; finish by making a loop knot and drawing it snug. Now take the shears and trim off any ragged moss not tied in smoothly, and the piece is ready for "ground-work."

FILLING THE DESIGN.

In starting this work, still using the wreath for illustration (see cut, page 19), select your ferns and place them in water; cut your smilax in short lengths and stem on three-quarter length tooth-picks; stem some leaves of the Mountain of Snow geranium, setting the pick up under the leaves; stem also 100 to 125 white carnations, three-quarter length stems, for solid work. Have also prepared quite a handful of begonia metallica leaves. With your mossed wreath in hand, fill in first your stemmed bunches of smilax, inserting the tooth-picks *through* the tinfoil on the side. This edging of green should be well done, so that when the design is laid down flat, nothing can be seen of the tinfoil at a horizontal line. For the want of this precaution, the work of otherwise skillful florists has often lost its effect. When a casket is being carried into or out of a church or house, a ragged circle of moss, or even tinfoil with a cresting of flowers, is not an inspiring spectacle; ditto the under side of pillows. Over and next to the smilax place a line of Mountain of Snow geranium leaves, with the picks stuck into the sphagnum, resting on the outer and inner rim of the wreath.

Commence with your white carnations. Run an edge around about one-half to two-thirds of the circle; fill in, setting the flowers closely together, and forming an oval or round effect. Fill in the half of the remaining space with begonia metallica leaves, placing them in irregular positions as though growing closely together. You have now finished the "body" part, and the work is ready for "surface" work. Select twelve or fifteen roses, either Perle or Mermet. These should be chosen on account of their perfect form or color, and should range in size from full blown roses to a small bud. Take your smallest bud first, wire it skillfully by carrying your wire under the stem, bringing up one or two small green leaves in graceful position, at the same time; finish by wiring on a tooth-pick. Do the other roses the same way, grading the length of stem to suit position. Stem some lily of the valley, clustered in its foliage; some fern leaves of different varieties, adiantums and davallias, and we are ready to put the finishing touches on our work. Arrange the roses (see engraving) in a loose crescent wreath on the begonia leaves, with the spray end of the roses falling gracefully over the carnations. Cluster your lily of the valley to the left; tie in a sash of white satin ribbon, No. 16 or 20. Add your ferns, using larger fronds under, and fine sprays over. A choice, delicate bit of fern produces an elegant touch in work that can be obtained by no other means.

A more commonplace arrangement is the wreath on page 17. This is made of mixed flowers, and suits a time when a cheap design must be prepared and you have run out of flowers. No. 7, on page 21, is formed mainly of roses, a few carnations, lily of the valley, fern leaves and smilax, and is a specimen wreath, as turned out of many floral stores.

SUGGESTIONS TO THE FLORIST WORKER.

Time is a most important factor in the making up of all floral designs, and he who wishes to succeed must learn to work rapidly. Care and study must be given to *all* the details. The fine touches denote the finished workman. Harmony of color must prevail—blues and purples never were known to combine. Blue pinks and purple pinks are difficult to use, and will harmonize with very few flowers. Many of our asters, sweet peas and hybrid roses come under this head. Light, delicate tints of pink and yellow, combined with white, suit the majority of tastes, and are safer for the young florist to commence with. For richer combinations there are Perle and Jacq. roses, Buttercup and Crimson King carnations; E. G. Hill, Lady Emma or Garfield carnations also all combine well with yellow. Strong contrasts *or* delicate shading should prevail; not an indefinite mixture. Lavender or purple combined with white, to be used at the funeral of elderly persons, is usually a successful combination.

Massing of color is a much more satisfactory arrangement than dotting it through the work.

Selected foliage is another matter of importance; a veiling of lace-like ferns thrown over a basket of roses is often the loveliest feature of the arrangement. Adiantum decorum is admirable for this purpose.

Adaptability of design to the occasion, or purpose required: Have some thought, idea or sentiment which you are developing, and your work will soon be idealized. *Individuality* is especially to be commended when it is combined with and governed by good taste.

But idealization can be carried to a point where it is ludicrous, as in the case of a wealthy old bachelor and an old maid, who were married in a prominent church. A unique affair was designed, consisting of two hearts, hung separately over the heads of the contracting parties on a system of wires, which were manipulated by the florist in charge, who was ensconced behind the pulpit. As the officiating minister pronounced the words which made the couple one, the two hearts slowly vibrated along the wire until they met, when only one blood red heart was visible! To say there was merriment in that church is to express it mildly. It dominated all the other features of the wedding.

The better class of florists are endeavoring to raise the standard of that class of work denominated "emblems." So many grotesque things have been perpetrated under that name, so deficient in all that pertains to good taste, that the better class of patrons in our large cities are demanding a simpler blending of floral ideas. Yet emblems and designs will be to a larger share of our population *the thing to have*, for some time to come, and it behooves us to get up these in the best manner we are capable of, giving our patrons good work, and keeping apace and ahead of our customers in floral taste. Be original, but study adaptability. Educate your customers to your standard, rather than to theirs, and in the long run it will pay in dollars and cents, as confidence will soon be established in your ability to produce new and meritorious work.

REQUISITES AND CONVENIENCES FOR WORK.

For the sake of convenience, we have placed together the necessary materials required. They consist of the following:

No. 36 iron annealed wire.
" 22 " "
" 20 " "

Pine tooth-picks, pointed both ends, 2,500 in a box.
Match-sticks, five to six inches long, in bundles of 100.
Linen thread, unbleached, Nos. 8 to 25.
Sphagnum, in barrels or bales.
Green moss, in sheets.
Tinfoil, in one pound packages.
Pair tweezers, to use where it is impossible to use fingers.
Scollay's sprinkler, for spraying.
Wire shears, and small shears for cutting ribbons, etc.

The wire comes in coils (usually a "stone" of twelve pounds), wrapped in strong heavy paper to protect it from moisture. And, right here, allow me a word of caution. Some florists have a habit, when opening a new coil of wire, of taking out what they need for immediate use, and hanging the balance on a convenient nail or peg. The moisture which is inseparable from all florists' places soon condenses, and in a short time the wire is covered with rust.

When No. 36 wire is rusty, it is spoiled for wrapping flowers. A good way is to have a wire box, with one or two trays or drawers in it large enough to contain two or more stones of wire ; these can be divided into compartments so as to allow wires already cut into lengths to be placed therein. Florists' places, as a rule, are very poorly equipped in regard to such conveniences. Again and again have we seen boxes of cut wires, covered with rust, mixed up with rusty nails of assorted sizes—perhaps a few odd suspender buttons! Again, string, wire and thread were in inextricable confusion. No paying business is conducted on this basis. Have your things neat and orderly if you expect to *make money out of the business.*

CHAPTER II.

PERSONAL AND SOCIAL FLORAL WORK.

Corsage Bouquets—Hand Bouquets—Dress Garnitures—Baskets. Flat and Handled Fans.

CORSAGE BOUQUETS or bunches are usually arranged in a loose, careless manner, but should not be wanting in grace. Always endeavor to find out what color of dress your bouquet is to be worn with, so as to intelligently determine what color of flower will be best to advise. Knowing this you will probably be able to suggest a combination that will thoroughly please your customer.

The following hints may contain something of use:

La France and Duchess de Brabant roses and fern leaves.

Papa Gontier roses and pink sweet peas of the same shade.

Mignonette and daffodils ; Mad. Cusin roses and pink bouvardias.

Mermet and rosy Roman hyacinths ; Niphetos roses and white Roman hyacinths.

Bride roses and lily of the valley ; Safrano roses and freesias.

Bon Silene roses and bleached sea moss, (one writer calls this " mermaid's hair ") ; carnations of sorts, with their own foliage.

Water lilies are best with no foliage. For "garden" corsage, we may have bunches of nasturtiums, geranium, golden rod, mignonette and sweet peas. Asparagus tenuissimus will not wilt, and with asparagus plumosa makes lovely misty green effects.

Two or three selected hybrid roses, such as Rothschild and Magna Charta, with a few buds, make a charming corsage for a matron. White necklaces and square fronts of marguerites, lily of the valley and Roman hyacinths, are lovely for young girls. Flowers with heavy fragrance should not be used, or used very sparingly.

HAND BOUQUETS.

These can consist of much the same combinations as were suggested for corsage purposes. No great admixture of colors or flowers is allowed by the present fancy. All hand bouquets are tied with ribbon ; the present fashion calls for 1¼ to 1½ yards of No. 12 to 16 ribbon as being the "correct" thing in width and length. Taste differs and fashions change in this, as in other matters of floral wear.

For bridal bouquets see Wedding Decorations, Chapter IV.

Besides the corsage combinations, the following maybe of use :

Bouquets of shaded pink roses, Papa Gontier and Bon Silene, shaded to blush buds of Camille, fringed with pale sweet peas and fern leaves.

Bouquet of Spiral mignonette, center cypripediums.

Bouquets of American Beauty or other roses, or violets, or orchids, interspersed with fern leaves (see engraving, page 85), or bouquets of two colors, as Catherine Mermet and W. F. Bennett, Perle des Jardins and Niphetos, La France and lily of the valley or Roman hyacinths.

For mourning, use a bunch of lily of the valley with border of Faust pansies, black or white ribbon ; or for lighter mourning a bouquet of white asters, shaded to purple edge, with ribbon to match. Some shades of lavender sweet peas are excellent for this work. Dark purple pansies and Niphetos roses also are good.

DRESS GARNITURES.

Young girls wear necklaces of marguerites sewed on white or black velvet ribbon, with square or V-shaped fronts of the same. Lily of the valley, sweet peas, Roman hyacinths, or any small blossoms are also suitable.

Bonnets covered with sweet peas, or field daisies, or clover and ferns, or variegated ivy geranium, have all been successfully made. "Lotta" wore on the stage a bonnet of white violets with a cluster of pink roses at the side. A front panel of lily of the vally on fine silver wire, made into a square mesh or lattice work over white satin, was used for a bride. For the same purpose, small white Roman hyacinths, white lilac, pea blossoms, or any other fine white flower could be used.

For party use, rose colored girdles of Mermet or Duchess de Brabant roses, or other pink flowers, are available ; any wearing flower can be made in this fashion. For a matron, a dark green silk, caught up with clusters of English ivy and heads of wheat, was effective. Another was of black lace, made up over lavender silk and and looped with a cluster of lavender-tinted asters ; a garland of the same crossed the floral breadth of the dress, and a bouquet of asters gave the finishing touch. An ecru silk was decorated with yellow ox-eyed daisies. Asparagus tenuissimus and plumosus are also valuable, for they do not wilt.

All flowers to be used for this purpose should be well soaked—that is, allowed to stand in water long enough to absorb all the water they will before using.   Freshly cut flowers will not stand.

BASKETS, FLAT AND HANDLED.

Baskets come now in innumerable shapes and styles, and are classified as flat and handled.   They are suitable for presentation as gifts, or wedding occasions, school commencements, for party and for theatre flowers.

A chaste arrangement for wedding was of white moss rosebuds, narcissus poeticus and fern leaves.

A flat basket was filled only with pink Cottage Maid tulips.

A handled basket of cardinal satin contained silvery rex begonias, choice fern leaves, and asparagus plumosus.

A yellow satin basket contained daffodils and the misty asparagus.

A grand combination is Baroness Rothschild or Capt. Christy roses and white orchids, or a basket filled entirely of white and tinted lilacs, with ribbon to match.   The following are all good : Mermet roses and forget-me-nots ; Roman hyacinths and Perle roses ; marguerites, ferns and Bon Silene roses ; pink bouvardia and pink roses, valance of pink satin, ribbon of the same shade on handle ; basket of violets, one-half white, and one-half blue, set with their own foliage.

Yellow roses (Perle), and white chrysanthemums ; Bride roses, ferns and smilax.   Hampers of shaded pansies, yellow and purple, with fern leaves, are lovely.

A cardinal trimmed basket, filled with Perle roses and yellow pansies.

A basket suitable for a progressive euchre prize could be made of white carnations, with a diamond center of Bon Silene roses.

For a grand basket, nothing can surpass a large flat basket, filled with long-stemmed hybrid roses—stems 15 to 17 inches long.   Heavily fringe such a basket with rose leaves and good fern leaves, and it is fine.

Another very different effect is produced by filling a handled basket with Lord Beaconfield pansies (blue, shaded) with a few trusses of wistaria interspersed   Arrange a graceful spray of Marechal Neil or Perle roses, and fasten this to the handle with a pretty knot of yellow ribbon the exact shade of the roses.   Pink roses for the yellow ; white for funeral purposes.

This list could be extended indefinitely, but the arrangements offered will suggest many other combinations.

FANS.

These are sometimes carried, but are generally on easels.   They are a favorite gift from a gentleman to a lady.   A fan on an easel of smilax is shown on page 73.

A pretty fan was edged with "sticks" of blue and white hyacinths ; a graceful spray of La France roses was laid on the open fan, and it resembled a hand-painted white satin fan with ostrich feathers at a short distance.   For descriptions of other fans, see cuts on pages 73 and 75.

CHAPTER III.

DECORATIVE EFFECTS.

General Suggestions—House Decorations—Hall Decorations—Mantel Decorations—Draperies and Screens—Effects with Ice.

IN THIS WORK plants in pots are one of the prime requisites. "I want plenty of large decorative plants" is almost the first thing your customer tells you ; after that, smilax, and then designs, draperies, etc., *ad libitum*—or rather, as you get paid for them.

HOUSE DECORATIONS.

In house decoration you must harmonize with the interior, and conceal any unpleasant object, bringing out anything of beauty and merit. Here the real artist is available, and will have his services in demand. Make your work either primary or secondary to the furnishings, for instance : a group of areca lutescens placed around and back of a large marble statue, or any fine piece of carving, greatly enhances the beauty of it by contrast. In this case the plants are made secondary, but the result is highly agreeable. Mantels, mirrors and stairways all offer special opportunities to the observant decorator.

HALL DECORATIONS.

The following suggestions may be useful :

Decorate a house with one kind of flower, for instance, roses ; pink in one room, yellow in another, white in another, and so on. Where roses are scarce, substitute any flower that is to be obtained in sufficient quantity. Daisy or marguerite decorations are popular. Pansies, gladiolus, lilies, water lilies or chrysanthemums can generally be obtained so that large decorations can be made of them.

Hall decorations require to be of coarser materials. The ceilings being higher, fine green would not be appreciated. Ground pine and laurel wreathing would, no doubt, be quite as satisfactory. In banking plants, it is a mistake to make one general line of miscellaneous varieties; instead, distribute your bright crimson and yellow foliage so as to brighten your groups of darker green; or better still, mass your brighter colors at one or two central points. Individualize your fine specimens by raising them above the others, or placing them by themselves. In the latter case, a covering of the pot is necessary. A simple and yet effective way of doing this, is to cover the pot smoothly with fine cotton batting; fasten this by tying a ribbon of some harmonious color around the pot; now give a "touch" by drawing through the knot one or two rose buds and foliage, or any flower that will tone with the ribbon. Tissue paper may be cut into strips and used in place of ribbon when expenditures have to be considered.

MANTEL DECORATIONS.

For a mantel with mirror, frame the mirror with rex begonia leaves, with plants of the same grouped to the right side of mantel. Take lilium auratum stems with flowers and buds, and plants of graded heights; with these plants and cut stems form a large crescent from the top of the glass to nearly the floor. Place adiantum ferns and lycopodium in pots; across the mantel on this arrange water lilies so they are all reflected in the mirror. Bank large ferns in the grate so to make a mass of green from mantel to floor, and your lily mantel is finished. Arches of lilies and ferns are very decorative.

A crimson-furnished room would be lovely in Perle roses and wheat, combined, or any other yellow flower, such as calendulas, chrysanthemums, tulips, pansies, etc. Any yellow foliage could also be well added.

An elaborate arrangement consisted of an open fire-place with "flames" of red flowers, presumably the tritoma, over which was hung an old-fashioned tea-kettle of chrysanthemums. The fender and fire-set were formed of yellow blossoms, and the tongs and shovel of marigolds.

A rose mantel is formed by filling the mantel with long-stemmed roses, forming them into vines up and around the mirror, allowing sprays and tendrils of the main vine to fall down and reflect in the mirror.

DRAPERIES AND SCREENS.

Curtain draperies in doorways, arches or windows, if smilax or asparagus, are often draped back with bunches of roses or carnations. Mirrors are sometimes treated the same way, with draperies of smilax for the foundation and roses, either La France, Perle, Safrano or Mermet, fastened on this foundation, making a rose curtain. Draperies of snowballs, syringa and sweet peas can also be made on fine wire. Asparagus and roses are an excellent combination. (See decorated mirror on page 83.)

Screens and panels are often desirable to shut off or screen some undesirable object. Screens may be of ivy with designs in flowers—for instance, a vase against a panel, as illustrated on page 97. I use ivies trained on square flat wire trellises, some four feet high ; these are very useful, as they can be used as trellises or panels, or to form a hedge or background for effective grouping.

A three-panel screen was formed of white pansies, with spray of Jean Liabaud roses for the first panel ; blue pansies, with cluster of pink moss roses and peach blossoms for the second ; and yellow pansies, with Paul Neyron roses and asparagus tenuissimus for the third.

Where rooms are small and space limited, tall palms may be placed in corners, and with the ivy plant screen will take up but little room. Lattice work of smilax, ivy or flowers, can be used in the upper part of doorways with or without curtains of smilax below.

EFFECTS WITH ICE.

In summer decorations ice can be used to good advantage ; a square crystal block placed where the water can drain off, and surrounded by palms, ferns or flowers, produces a cooling sensation when a day is close and warm. Or, it can be ice in the centre of a little pool, with water lilies, ferns, daisies and violets growing on the surrounding bank. A pyramid of ice, with colored lights inside, forms a pretty fairy grotto, which should have tall-growing ferns surrounding it.

CHAPTER IV.

WEDDING WORK.

THE REGULATION BRIDAL BOUQUET is formed either of Bride or Niphetos roses or lily of the valley, or if it can be afforded, orchids, and tied with from 2½ to 3½ yards of ribbon, No. 12 or 16. The suggestions offered in Chapter II will apply here.

Page 85 illustrates a beautiful bride's bouquet in which the roses were Bride, with adiantum ferns.

Bridesmaid's bouquets are of the same kind of flowers, but smaller, and are either all of one color or different colors of one kind of flowers. The sash should correspond with the color of the bouquet.

Bridesmaids also carry satchels, pockets or sun hats, suspended from the arm by ribbons; these can be filled with roses, sweet peas, Roman hyacinths or water lilies. Children sometimes carry wreaths of Roman hyacinths, Mignonette (Polyantha) roses, or lily of the valley.

Bride's dresses are garnitured with natural flowers. Front panels of lily of the valley, forming fringe; network of the same made on silver wire, as well as garlands, are employed. V-shaped necks are finished with clusters of roses, or orange blossoms if they can be obtained.

WEDDING BOWERS.

A bay window, a corner of a room, or in front of a mantel are the places usually chosen in which to arrange floral bowers. Mirrors add much to the effectiveness of the work. Where possible, obtain them and line the interior of the bay or background with them; conceal the frames with plants, smilax, ferns, etc.

A ceiling effect, in this case, will be good. A bough of dogwood, or a simulated bough of smilax, white chrysanthemums or even carnations will answer. Canopies are not used as much as formerly, other designs taking their place.

For suspended designs, we have Bells, Lovers' Knots, Monograms, Four-leaved Clovers, Wish-bones, Hooks and Eyes, Horse-shoes, Yokes, Balls, Parasols (representing protection), Lock and Key (emblemizing marriage), Horns of Plenty, etc., to choose from. For Bow and Arrow, Lovers' Knot and Horse-shoe, see pages 91, 87 and 71 respectively. Other arrangements can consist of a monogram, one letter in white, and the other in pink or scarlet flowers; or a bow-knot, formed of marguerites with long loops and ends; a clover-leaf, filled with white carnations or lily of the valley; a wish-bone of Bride or Jacqueminot roses; hook and eye of white carnations or chrysanthemums; horse-shoe of white carnations, with crescent arrangement of La France roses, instead of lilies and pansies (see page 71). Any one of these designs can be used in connection with the bower. Bank plants around the sides and base of your mirrors, and this part of your work is complete.

Garlands of flowers are sometimes used very effectively. Large flowers, such as hybrid roses, pansies, gladiolus, tulips and hydrangeas, are especially adapted for a showy decoration. Small flowers do not count in this work. Silver draperies, of silver cloth, fringed with lily of the valley, caught back with clusters of the same, make an ideal chaste arrangement for a wedding. An arrangement of this kind was also used at a silver wedding, and, in place of lily of the valley, ivy leaves covered with frosted silver were used. This picture was thrown into strong relief by clumps of dark green palms which stood on either side. Other forms of the bower are also used, as also a simulated tent, the front gable of a house, and other ideas too numerous to mention—anything within the limit of good taste is permissible in a wedding decoration, and judicious originality is in demand.

OTHER ACCESSORIES.

Among other floral accessories, hassocks of flowers have been used; rugs of flowers to kneel on; wedding wreaths of pink roses, tied with ribbon of the same.

An "old-fashioned" decoration could be made of marigolds, candy-tuft, hollyhocks, deutzias, buttercups, mignonette, pinks and daisies, arranged with grasses and placed in old-fashioned vases and jars.

Golden wedding decorations consist largely of golden or yellow blossoms. The two dates of the wedding is a popular device, as 1838—1888, The figures can be made of buttercups, carnations, Perle roses, or ivy leaves covered with frosted gold. Monograms are appropriate and pretty formed of yellow and white flowers. Golden cornucopias of chrysanthemums, pouring forth golden blossoms, have been used successfully, and are very rich in effect.

CHURCH DECORATIONS.

Here the grouping of plants and other floral work should be made secondary features of the occasion. If possible, be on hand at the "practice" the night before, and indicate on the floor the position of the bridesmaids and the ushers. Plan your plant decoration to form a background, and supplement the grouping of the wedding party. Place your palms and dark green-leaved plants in such a position that they will "bring out" the white bridal dresses, leaving the brighter-leaved plants to heighten the contrast with the sober black worn by the gentlemen. If your price is limited, do not try to scatter over too much space—better group your effects. If given "carte-blanche," bank in heavily, being careful to give prominence to what fine specimens you may have. A number of good large evergreens in pots, of choice kinds, will help out wonderfully on a cold day decoration, when choice stuff would be ruined by taking out of the houses. The only designs allowable at church decorations are a simple arch of lilies or a large flat basket of white flowers, or a large vase filled with Niphetos roses. Smilax can be draped over the altar rail and other features of the church furniture.

CHAPTER V.

MEMORIAL AND FUNERAL DESIGNS.

Designs for Infants—For Young Persons—For the Prime of Life; Ladies—For the Prime of Life; Men—For Aged People—Special Funeral Designs—Military and G. A. R. Designs—Society and Lodge Designs—Inscriptions for Memorial Designs.

ALL FLORISTS are frequently called upon to prepare these silent tributes of love and esteem for the dead. Such work demands our best efforts.

For the sake of convenience, we have sub-divided the funeral work into classes suitable for different ages.

DESIGNS FOR INFANTS.

Simplicity must be the key-note—everything sweet and lovely, but nothing gaudy. White is childhood's own color. Use fine, fragile blossoms, not large—an absence of large flowers should distinguish this class of work.

The selection of suitable arrangements is limited. The following is a partial list: If a very small baby, the best way is to lay it out in flowers. To do this, it is necessary to go to the house and arrange your work there. Place some delicate ferns, or even smilax, for foundation ; arrange in effective relief against this Mignonette roses, lily of the valley or sweet peas and rose buds—any fine white flower will answer.

The cover of one of these little caskets was formed entirely of freesia, with the name of the little one in blue forget-me-nots. Another was a cradle of blossoms with the little one laid in it, with a cover-lid of white cashmere covered with Roman hyacinths, the corner turned back and faced with marguerites ; an exquisite fringe of lily of the valley finished this beautiful receptacle for the baby's last sleep.

Wreaths of marguerites, wreaths of small roses; stars of the same, and of mixed flowers, will always be called for.

An outer casket formed entirely of carnations and rose buds is a chaste design; the cover of the same bearing a crescent wreath of lily of the valley and white violets, tied with a narrow satin ribbon. Sometimes only the cover is made of flowers, with a garland around the lower edge of casket.

For pillows and other designs suitable for inscriptions we suggest, " My Baby;" " Asleep in Jesus ;" " Safe in the Arms of Jesus ;" " He Knoweth Best ;" " Suffer Little Children to Come Unto Me."

Chaste offerings are basket of white roses with dove fluttering over clusters of forget-me-nots ; a crescent cluster, either of white roses tied with white ribbon, or blush roses tied with ribbon of the same shade. Primroses, Roman hyacinths and lily of the valley can all be effectively employed. Harps of pure white are also called for.

Sometimes has been used a rug of white carnations, fringed with sweet peas, white begonias, or Roman hyacinths. The infant's casket rested on a bier or mound of sweet alyssum and white roses, which stood on the mat of blossoms. Again, the casket can be placed among field daisies and ferns.

DESIGNS FOR YOUNG PERSONS.

In these a little more color may appear, but it will give the best results to confine the choice of colors to very delicate tints.

A simple wreath is made of mixed flowers or Safrano roses, white carnations, and pansies. Very pretty is the crescent wreath, formed only of Niphetos and adiantum ferns, tied with satin ribbon ; or, use white violets and blue forget-me-nots ; or, an oval wreath of white carnations and pale Mermet roses with a veiling of adiantum ferns. A name can be made through the center of this. (See pages 19 and 21.)

A delicate wreath is formed of eucharis and lily of the valley ; and a beautiful crescent wreath was of blue forget-me-nots, on which was arranged a bunch or cluster of white roses.

A cross of pale pink and white moss rose-buds, with a base of silvery rex begonia leaves, is suitable for a young girl. A standing square cross of white carnations, springing from a rocky base among fern leaves, with a climbing " vine " of roses (either Perle or Niphetos), is valuable for a young man ; for a lady use Mermet or white roses.

A broken column with silver drapery is elegant. Form the shaft of carnations, packed closely together to give the effect of marble; the broken-off top lay on the base. For a 35-inch column, three-quarters of a yard of silver cloth will be sufficient, and enough silver fringe of a simple pattern to cross both ends of drapery. The full width of the material will be necessary to drape it properly. Sew the fringe on opposite sides of the cloth, because when you drape it you throw one end up over. To arrange it, drape in statuesque folds ; throw over one end, and allow it to fall in classic outlines. If this is well handled, it is a beautiful addition. Use no color with this design, and you will be surprised at its chaste beauty. If price will allow, have column stand on double square base formed of solid white carnations, the edges clearly outlined. "Broken Hopes" would be an appropriate inscription if lettering is desired, but it is better without.

A fine arrangement is a draped pall of white blossoms, sewed on white cashmere or silesia, with a fringe of lily of the valley or white begonias. This should be gracefully draped over the foot of the casket, being caught up with bunches of rose-buds, lilies or some other flowers to keep it in place.

A large handled basket of white water liles, with a dove suspended in a fluttering position, is effective.

A fine wreath is made on a single wire, weaving in Roman hyacinths and fern leaves ; tie with ribbon. This is best in a crescent form, and is simple but lovely. A wreath of lily of the valley can be treated the same way, with a cluster of long-stemmed Niphetos roses.

DESIGNS FOR THE PRIME OF LIFE—LADIES.

A wreath : single white azaleas, set closely together, forming a fluffy, fringy, wreath ; fasten to one side a cluster of Roman hyacinths, lily of the valley or roses : tie with ribbon. If for an older lady, use heliotrope, pansies, purple orchids, lavender ribbon and fern leaves. Another beautiful wreath is made by using chrysanthemum La Frizure which has been grown inside and which is like fringed silk ; finish by fastening choice flowers as formerly described.

A cross and wreath combined ; cross of Mermet roses and wreath of any white flowers.

A cross and crown ; cross of Jacqueminot roses and crown of heliotropes.

A wreath of pink roses, with a cross of callas or blue pansies.

A wreath of pale pink, with a heart inside, made of either of crimson roses or blue violets.

Anchor of camellias and lily of the valley or candytuft, with two clusters of roses and ferns at intersection of arms.

The most beautiful Gates Ajar I ever saw was entirely of white, with garlands of white roses around the posts. A white dove was so placed as to appear in the darkened room to be taking his flight to heaven with a soul in his charge. This can be gotten up in a magnificent manner, but is easily spoiled in the hands of a poor workman.

Pillows can be formed of solid white, with crescent wreath of pink roses, or of fern leaves, with crescent wreath of water lilies or lilium candidum. Work the name in white double primroses or carnations ; or white chenille or immortelles will do well for lettering.

A pillow may be of La France roses, with cross of lily of the valley in center ; or a pillow of ivy leaves, with sickle of white roses on the ivy ; or a pillow with two diagonal corners filled with lilies, center panel of white carnations, name in violets, fringing of ferns.

Crown of golden roses—Perle and Neil—with fern leaves.

Lyre of white azaleas and roses, with carnations.

Star of violets, with lily of the valley for points, eucharis in center ; pink rose, Roman hyacinths and lilium candidum could be used for the same purpose.

Standing cross of white carnations and ivy (friendship) growing up and over it ; base of fern and begonia leaves.

Holy Bible—open Bible on cushion, with sickle holding the book open ; the book bound in fine green sea moss. Or a Bible with cross of Safrano buds laid on the open page is good. The Bible is supposed to be open at the record of deaths ; the name and age are placed on left page, and small lettering must be used.

A Grecian urn of white carnations, with garland of pink or yellow roses, makes a suitable design.

A basket cover was made in two parts, leaving an oval space for the name plate. It was made of white carnations, set evenly together with an edging of fern leaves. A wreath of pale pink roses, with clusters of lily of the valley and foliage, completed it.

A young bride who had passed away was laid out in this way : The white casket lay in front of a mirror and mantel. A mass of silver drapery nearly hid the mirror from sight, falling to the floor and being draped around the casket, so as to enclose the bier in its folds. A rich pall of lily of the valley, made without foliage and sewed on white cashmere, was draped over the foot of the open casket. A standing cross of eucharis, lily of the valley and white roses stood on the mantel and emerged from between the folds of the silver drapery. Laid over the base was a ribbon bearing the inscription, "We Look Beyond the Cross." At the head stood a table of flowers bearing an Open Book of Life—the last two pages of her life, 21 and 22, were in the left and right corners respectively. "Finis," showed the last page had been reached, while a spray of white rose buds lay in the center of the left hand page ; passing under this and laying diagonally across the pages was a white satin book-mark : with the inscription in gold leaf "He Chasteneth Us." A Gates Ajar stood at the foot, and was sent by her Sunday-school class. A dove fluttered on his perch over the gates, bearing in his bill this message of peace. "Awake into Life Eternal." She lay on one side, with her hand under her cheek, as though sleeping sweetly her last sleep.

DESIGNS SUITABLE FOR THE PRIME OF LIFE—MEN.

Quiet, rich colors should prevail. Ivy designs are deservedly popular, and are really elegant where good taste is employed in their "get up." All ivy leaves should be polished before using; this is easily done by rubbing them with a brush or cloth dipped in a little sweet-oil.

An ivy cross: a standing ivy cross with Niphetos or Perle roses in vine form, running up and drooping over the arms in careless tendrils; clusters of lily of the valley, Roman hyacinths and other graceful blossoms may be arranged as though growing on base.

For ivy wreaths, lay your leaves one overlapping the other, but give a little variety to the position, so as to avoid a "set" appearance. On this place a crescent spray of purple pansies; tone with fine fern leaves.

In an ivy column, the leaves must be of medium size, and set closely together. The "break off" at the top should be filled with heliotrope, violets or pansies; if no other flowers can be had, purple immortelles will answer. White chenille, white immortelles, cape flowers, double primroses or carnations all make good lettering for ivy work.

A fine broken column was of ivy, with an anchor of white flowers, to which was attached a golden chain of jonquils. A harp or lyre with broken strings can be substituted for the anchor.

A scroll, or roll of honor, of ivy leaves, with inscription or with cross and crown, as on page 35, is very effective. A cross of eucharis, calla or candidum lilies is lovely in this design; in fact, any design shows to good advantage in contrast with the dark green of the ivy.

Gates ajar of white flowers, with base of ivy and fern leaves, is very chaste and handsome. Other rich arrangements are:

A pall of black pansies, sewed on black cashmere and caught up with crossed palm leaves, on which may be laid a bunch of white lilies.

Ivy pillows, with short inscriptions, such as "Father" or "Husband," in carnations or smaller lettering, in white; or a sickle of Niphetos roses, with handle of purple Dutch hyacinths. Either wreath or cross are beautiful in white lilies, roses, etc.

For men, more color is permissible, as a wreath of Jacqueminot or American Beauty roses, veiled with fine fern leaves, laid on crossed palm leaves; a standing cross of Jacqueminot roses and lily of the valley; pillow of same, with cross of the latter flower.

Make a casket-cover of black bronze or purple pansies; form a garlands of the same, and drape around the coffin.

Basket of Perle roses and purple hyacinths; or a large flat basket of mignonette, Perle roses and Mermets. A wreath may be of oak leaves (denoting strength), with a branch of laurel.

A pall of dark purple velvet; drape with a few graceful sprays of passion vine, with flowers and buds.

Palm leaves (victory), crossed with large cluster of Puritan roses, with sash of ribbon. Palm leaves, entwined with choice cattleyas.

Disabled steamship, with broken spars, laying on its side, stranded on a bank of fern leaves, with waves of blue hyacinths, blue ageratum or pansies.

Lyre of hybrid roses, with strings of purple chenille.

Hour-glass and scythe—the reaper of time.

Book of Life : arrange according to directions previously given (page 135), with the age of deceased. Suitable inscriptions for a man would be : "He Giveth His Beloved Sleep;" or, "I Know That My Redeemer Liveth ;" or, "He Giveth the Victory." Sometimes some simple quotation like above will carry more consolation to the sorrowing friends than all the flowers that could be arranged, and, believe me, when they need something again, they will come to you to get it! Other suitable designs have been described in connection with the illustrations.

DESIGNS SUITABLE FOR AGED PEOPLE.

These must be less pronounced, and be of dignified effect. Over-done work for aged people is as bad as it is for children. Suitable arrangements are :

A wreath of black pansies and heliotrope, or Marechal Niel roses and purple pansies.

A crown of violets ; pillow or cross of same. A wreath of wheat, with cluster of fern leaves and lavender ribbon.

A cross of black pansies, with a cluster of eucharis at the intersection of the arms. A wreath of cissus discolor, with spray of pale pink or white roses ; very distinct.

Four cycas leaves, arranged to form a wreath, with purple ribbon clustered under in short loops, and fastened with the same.

Pall of royal purple velvet, covered with cattleyas ; sickle of white roses and heliotrope laid on a flat sheaf of wheat.

A bier of purple asters, finished with myrtle ; a black velvet casket, trimmed with garlands of white roses.

Standing cross of ivy, with sickle of white roses, and sheaf of wheat on base of fern leaves. An ivy cross, with wheat wreath over the arms. A very expensive arrangement consisted of an entire casket of violets, with a crown of the same sweet flowers.

A pillow may be of violets, with inscription, "Asleep in the Lord ;" cluster of Perle roses and wheat in lower right hand corner ; ferns and smilax for backing.

A superb large wreath was made by cutting an ordinary thirteen inch wreath open on the ends ; two palm leaves were attached, and then heavy masses of Dutch hyacinths of an exquisite shade of lavender purple, with rich fern leaves. It was tied with a heavy satin sash of the same shade of purple.

A cluster of exquisite Bride roses was employed in one case. A wreath or draping of roses or violets is often hung over the pew of the deceased, in a church funeral.

A casket cover can also be made of violets, with a wreath of ivy or white roses laid on it. Star of violets ; cluster of eucharis in center.

Wreath of mignonette (with spikes all laid one way), wheat and purple pansies. Casket cover of purple asters; a cross of rich ferns. A wreath of asters and auratum lilies.

Sickle of graded Niphetos roses, made on single wire, using from five to eight dozen roses; back it with rose leaves and fine ferns. A sickle of ivy leaves, laid on flat sheaf of wheat; a loose, careless cluster of heliotrope or pansies laid at intersection of handle and blade; or, a sickle of all purple pansies. A sickle should only be used for old persons, as it emblemizes old age.

SPECIAL FUNERAL DESIGNS.

For an engineer: locomotive four feet long; boiler of white pinks and Niphetos roses; cab of Perle roses and candytuft; tender of lilies and roses, with smoke-stack of Perle buds.

For vice president of railway: A locomotive, cab and boiler of white roses and carnations; hand rails and pilot purple immortelles; headlight, red carnations; tender, white and yellow roses; purple track, crimson ties; road-bed of ferns, twelve feet in length. For same: A private car entering tunnel; car of white buds; tunnel of fern leaves, dotted with marguerites.

For a telegraph operator: two telegraph poles, with connecting line broken down, on field of ferns.

For a bookkeeper: a desk, with a sponge cup made of immortelles and flowers, with an unfinished manuscript on the lid of the desk. An open ledger of white carnations, eucharis, freesias and lily of the valley, laying upon a desk of ferns; a bookmark of satin ribbon contained the inscription, "Accounts Closed." A closed ledger with the word "ledger" on the cover, with pen laid on it, also can be used for the same purpose. The pen can be whittled out of a cycas leaf.

For a journalist: Desk of ivy; one corner, bunch of lily of the valley; inkstand of violets; quill pen, formed of a palm leaf; a vase of flowers with the inscription, "Last Copy Finished." A full sized sheet of newspaper, resting on an easel. The columns were separated by column rules of single lines of black immortelles; the columns were filled with sweet alyssum, which at a short distance resembled reading matter; the plain surface at the top of the page was of white carnations, with the name of the paper in black pansies. The outside edge was of single white azaleas set very closely together. A graceful garland, or drapery, of La France roses and buds formed a decoration over the left hand corner, and fell in careless sprays down the sides and up over the easel. "30" was lettered at the bottom of the sheet, meaning in newspaper parlance, *finis.* The easel was covered with smilax and ferns.

For musicians: A banjo of bronze pansies. A cornet of Perle roses, laid on bed of ferns. A guitar of alternanthera paronychoides major, laid on bed of white roses and carnations. A violin of white carnations and roses, with strings of purple or white chenille, broken. A bar of music, with notes formed of purple immortelles or violets. Lyres and harps are also appropriate for this purpose. A white yacht on sea of Roman hyacinths.

MILITARY AND G. A. R. DESIGNS.

These usually represent in some way the national colors, red, white and blue. The proportions of color depend on which branch of the service you are working for—blue indicates the infantry, red the artillery, and yellow the navy.

A military button : A white star of Niphetos roses, white balsams and carnations, was laid on a flat round basket. The spaces between the points were filled in, two points of red carnations, two points of yellow Perles and one point of blue " Bachelor's Buttons " or larkspur ; edged with ferns and smilax.

A pillow of Niphetos roses and pansies, upon which rested crossed swords of violets, entwined with a small laurel wreath.

A draped flag, in graceful folds of the red, white and blue. Red, of scarlet geraniums or carnations ; white, carnations or balsams, and blue, of immortelles or blue violets, pansies, larkspur, or " Bachelor's Buttons." The stars were of daisies.

A panel laid on an easel had a flag worked on it, the panel being of white flowers or ivy, and the flag made as above. A scroll of ivy leaves had laid on it a flag of the red, white and blue, which was caught into folds by a drawn sabre.

A star of blue violets or pansies on white ground is pretty.

An upright shield, standing on base of dark hybrid roses. The lower portion of shield was striped red (Jacqueminot) and white (Niphetos) roses ; the upper section of blue was of solid blue pansies, with stars of single blossoms of hydrangea Thomas Hogg.

The Garfield ladder of fame. This may suggest something for similar occasions. Placed at the base of the ladder is the canal boat, his starting point. He started climbing the ladder of fame at Chester ; continuing up we mark the next step Williams. Then followed his upward steps in military and political life—Colonel, General, Congressman, U. S. Senator and President. A crown surmounted the ladder, emblemizing the final upward step. The union shield, draped in mourning with a dove of peace resting on it, bearing in its beak the inscription on white satin, " In Memoriam."

A soldier's cap. A knapsack of white flowers, with monogram of company in red, white and blue.

A monument, surmounted with an eagle, bearing a streamer with " G. A. R." on it ; or, an eagle on shield of white. A stack of guns made of violets, on field of daisies and ferns.

Pen and sword entwined, with laurel wreath.

SOCIETY AND LODGE DESIGNS.

These mostly require emblematic colors also.

Maltese cross, made of Jacqueminot or Bennett roses, or scarlet carnations or geraniums. This may be varied by making a border of white flowers, the center of scarlet.

A Masonic Bible of white carnations, on a pulpit cushion of crimson flowers. The square and compass laid on the open page was made of violets.

Maltese cross on easel, with cross and crown in center, is the accepted Masonic design. The Maltese cross of red, the cross of Niphetos roses, the crown of Perle roses.

Banner of white, with cross and crown in center. The scroll of honor can also be used with this device ; see page 35. A banner of white carnations, with Maltese cross of Jacqueminot roses. Square and compass of white flowers. Letter G in scarlet, or square in white ; compass in blue and G in scarlet.

Knights of Pythias: A visor, crossed battle axes, or an eagle holding the inscription " K. of P." in its beak.

I. O. O. F. : Three links—one of Jacqueminot roses, one of Mermet and one of Perle ; or all white, with clusters of their colors where links cross. Crossed battle axes of white, or of violets on white ground. Star, with eye in center. A triangle or double triangle of blue and white ; or made of lilies, roses and assorted flowers.

Knights of Labor: A wreath with triangle in center.

United Workmen : Anchor and shield combined.

For a fireman : A hat or ladder, a fire engine, crossed axes, or a trumpet, are all applicable.

For policemen there can be made a badge, a belt, a club, and a helmet.

For druggist : Mortar and pestle.

Base ball player : Crossed bats, on a diamond field, with ball.

SUITABLE INSCRIPTIONS FOR MEMORIAL DESIGNS.

" We Look Beyond the Cross."   (Cross.)

" No Cross, No Crown."   (Cross.)

" Beyond the River."   (Pillow.)

" Gone Home."   (Gates Ajar or Pillow.)

" He Chasteneth Us."   (Bible.)

" The Lord's Will Be Done."   (Bible or Pillow.)

" Let not your heart be troubled."   (Bible.)

" Finis."   (Book of Life.)

" At Rest."

" Rest in Peace."

" Mother," " Father," " Sister," Brother."

" Faith," "Asleep," " Baby."
 Any proper names may also be used.
" All Is Well." (Pillow.)
"Simply to Thy Cross I Cling." (Cross on Rock.)
" Asleep in Jesus." (Young children.)
" Rock of Ages, Cleft for Me."
" Farewell."
" A Tribute of Friendship."
" In War Victorious ; In Peace Supreme."
" He Knoweth Best."
" The Link Broken Here Will be Joined Again in Heaven."
" I know that my Redeemer liveth."
" He Giveth His Beloved Sleep."
" Safe in the Arms of Jesus."
" Suffer little children to come unto me."
" Her children rise up and call her blessed."
" O death ! Where is thy sting? O grave ! Where is thy victory ? "
" I am the resurrection and the life."
" Christ Is My Hope." (Bible.)
" The Angels Called Her."
" The Morning Cometh." (Panel.)
" Of such is the kingdom of heaven." (Child.)
" Here I lay my burden down."
" Not Dead, But Gone Before."
" Broken Hopes." (Column.)
" The Lord giveth, the Lord taketh away."
" In Memory of ——— "
" In Memoriam."
" He Giveth The Victory."
" Awake Into Life Eternal."
" She Sleepeth."
" Asleep In The Lord."
" I go to prepare a place for you." (Bible.)

Chapter VI.

MISCELLANEOUS DESIGNS.

Exhibition Designs—Floral Oddities—Easter Decorations—Easter Cross—Easter Conceits—Christmas Decorations.

EXHIBITION DESIGNS admit of much variety. Any of the designs previously mentioned may be used, or the following may be suggestive.

Bridges built on foundations of alternantheras, the bridge proper being of flowers, and a large mirror underneath forming the waterway, with a bank of ferns around latter.

A large butterfly was effective, made on black velvet; the back of the insect of adiantum ferns, with the wings and spots on wings marked out by varied flowers.

A swan on basket; a gypsy kettle.

An elephant, whose body was composed of white carnations, with tusk of callas. A dirty-colored immortelle was also used successfully to produce a life-like representation of his elephantship.

Pedestal of white carnations and roses, surmounted by a vase of white carnations, with a garland of pink roses around the whole. A Japanese screen of chrysanthemums can be made very effective.

An archery target, on easel, with crossed arrows.

A butterfly, with body of pink carnations and roses, and wings of yellow. A large elk, full size, of white flowers.

Monkey of Faust pansies, climbing a miniature tree.

Owl and crescent. An owl and the new moon of echeveria (living plants) ; or, the moon of yellow roses and owl of white Cape flowers, white carnations or Faust pansies.

A horseshoe of fruit—grapes, oranges, split pears, etc. An acorn, signifying strength.

A bicycle of white roses, with seat of pink carnations. A suspended balloon, with car attached. A locomotive headlight. A capstone and anchor. A lamp-post and letter-box.

FLORAL ODDITIES.

These may be useful, and when properly handled are generally very effective.

A surprise bouquet is made of Perle roses, enclosed in cabbage leaves, to represent a huge cabbage.

A bouquet of American Beauty roses, with stems three feet long.

A column of blue hydrangeas, draped in greens, tied with watered green ribbon, and filled with sunflowers; it should be standing on a soap box, inscribed "*B. T. Babbitt's Best.*"

Spider and fly on a web; web of white Florida moss was stretched across poles ten feet in height. The body of his spidership was of Perle roses, striped with black pansies, heliotropes and maiden-hair ferns. The head was of La France roses, and the legs were of tuberoses strung on wires. The fly was composed of mixed flowers, and had wings of gauze.

A young lady who graduated from a dental college was presented by admiring friends with a floral tooth. A local correspondent in the *American Florist* says: "It was formed of white Cape flowers, and a lot of yellow immortelles did duty as gold filling. The tooth was a foot high, and created lots of merriment."

EASTER DECORATIONS.

To make an artistic success of these, symbolism of color should be studied. Red represents divine love; white, purity, faith and regeneration; blue, truth, constancy, holiness and fidelity. Purple and violet were the colors dedicated to royalty; green symbolizes hope of immortality and victory. The laws that govern harmony of color should always be kept in mind, whatever is done.

A fine Easter cross stood about eight feet high, and rose from a double square base. The cross was formed of calla lilies, lily of the valley and Roman hyacinths. The upper square of the base was of white carnations, and was 2½ feet square. (Cape flowers or immortelles could be used instead of carnations.) On each corner of the upper base a white dove was perched. A garland of blue forget-me-nots were held up by these four doves, while a profusion of Marechal Niel roses were grouped on one corner and had overflowed onto the green sub-base. This was formed of green moss, lycopodium and ferns. "He is Risen" was lettered in scarlet immortelles on the white groundwork of the upper base on the front panel.

A cross of white flowers, with a green base and a large cluster of scarlet cacti at the intersection of the arms, is rich and effective. Liliums Harrisii and candidum, and the calla lily, are the things *par excellence* for work at this time of the year.

A cross can be of white tulips, hyacinths and astilbe japonica, with base of daffodils and ferns.

EASTER CONCEITS.

A gilt egg, burst asunder, with crocuses, daisies, Roman hyacinths or any spring flower, is pretty for a gift, as also is a half egg shell, with downy chicks inside, nestled in a basket of Easter flowers.

Goslings poking their heads through the shells, the whole lying in a bed of flowers ; or a dozen eggs lying in a basket of flowers.

A novelty offered last year was white satin egg-shaped baskets, filled with pink roses and Roman hyacinths, blue violets and marguerites, or daffodils and jonquils, with ferns for each or any of them. The egg was bound with a white satin ribbon.

A dove of white flowers ; an owl of violets ; a wheelbarrow of lily of the valley and forget-me-nots, with an egg in the center.

CHRISTMAS DECORATIONS.

Christmas is now a greater day with the florists than New Year's day. Flowers are scarce and prices are high—too high. The ingenuity of the florist is taxed to the utmost to get out his orders in satisfactory shape. Instead of giving combinations such as would be used on ordinary occasions when we have plenty of flowers, I offer a few suggestions as to combining materials that can be obtained more readily than fresh flowers, and will aid in economizing the latter.

A Christmas cross (square) of bouquet green, stemmed and set closely together, trimmed off with the shears, with a wreath of red immortelles or holly around the arms. Holly could also be clustered on base. This would be suitable for a Sunday school or church.

A standing cross of lycopodiums, with clusters of Bennett, Mermet or white roses. This—the lycopodium cross—should be grown previously in the greenhouse. A lyre can also be made of the same, with lilies and roses in clusters, or an urn can also be used in the same way, with a garland drooped over it. The last few designs are also suitable for funerals.

We must not lose sight of Cape flowers—their utility can not be questioned. Designs of them can be prepared in slack times and kept on hand ; then when in a tight place for flowers, bring out your wreaths or crosses, describe in glowing terms the beauty obtained by a cluster or two of roses and fern leaves added to the Cape flower work, and you generally get the order. Ribbon, judiciously employed, helps out greatly in a scarcity of flowers. Talk "plenty of green :" show them smilax designs, ivy designs, fern designs "livened with clusters"—anything to "tide over" the scarcity and bring in a few dollars for yourself, instead of the commission man in the cities, during the season of high prices.

Of course if first-class patrons are willing to pay for good work, they must have it ; but I am now talking of the great mass of customers who are not willing to pay the higher prices demanded at Christmas, and who if they do of necessity buy flowers at way-up prices, will generally remember it against you, although you may not have made anything on the work yourself.

For decorating in houses, smilax, holly and ground pine wreathing are desirable. Use the wreathing for outlining with smilax for lighter touches. A lattice-work design of holly for over doors, or over the upper part of mirrors, will be good, as also horse-shoes of the same, with berries arranged in clusters, similar to arrangement on page 71.

For dark wall papers, snow and frost effects are lovely. They are produced by spreading tufts of cotton batting over evergreen boughs and decorating in whatever way desired. Sprinkle the cotton with " diamond " dust.

Mottoes and texts are demanded for church decorations, such as : " Glory to God in the highest, and on earth peace, good will toward men ;" " Hosanna to the son of David ;" " Alleluia ;" " God is Love ;" " Glory be to God on high ;" " Thou art the King of Glory ;", " Unto us a Child is born, unto us a Son is given ;" " Behold ! thy King cometh." These can be made of bouquet green, holly or evergreens ; or, make the letters of paste-board, cover with white cotton, and sprinkle with frosting ; place them against a background of evergreen sprigs, or other dark surface.

For other ideas : A star of holly, with wreath of red immortelles in center ; a flat star of red with a crown of Cape flowers. Solid wreaths of red immortelles are good for bits of brilliant coloring.

Laurel wreathing, and palm leaves from the South, are admirable for large decorations, and help out on the plant question exceedingly. No florist likes to expose his choice palms and plants to injury at this season of the year unless he is well paid for it. Evergreens in pots, planted in early fall and wintered in a cold house where frost does not enter, make a good substitute. Aucuba Japonica is also decidedly useful, as cold does not affect it much.

CHAPTER VII.

FLOWERS FOR SPECIAL OCCASIONS.

Dinner Parties— June Table—Pink Dinner—Conch Shell Decoration—Yachting Luncheon —Pea Blossom Luncheon—Sea-Foam Dinner— Chrysanthemum Dinner—Christening Gifts.

FLOWERS AT DINNER PARTIES are very popular in our large cities, and the professional florist is taxed to the utmost to evolve something new in this line of work. The following may suggest something to the exhausted brain worker.

June table : Large plateau of Jacqueminot roses ; delicate green foliage of ferns and asparagus tenuissimus. Corsage bouquets of the same, tied with watered sea green ribbon. Boutonieres alternated with these at the different plates.

Pink dinner : Sweet peas of delicate shade of pink, Mermet and Duchess de Brabant roses were used in this case.

A yellow arrangement was of croton leaves, combined with filling of Perle roses, tied with satin ribbon to match. A scarf of the same golden shade of silk was laid diagonally across the table, with sprays of golden pansies arranged as vines laid carelessly on it.

Conch shell decoration : A large suspended conch shell hung over the table from the chandelier, draped lightly with smilax, intertwined with lengths of asparagus. The shell was filled with drooping pink begonias and Mermet roses. Smaller shells were placed at the plates on little stands, and were used as finger bowls, each filled at one side with a cluster of pink begonias and roses.

A sea green scarf was laid on the table, on which was placed a large silver dish, containing water lilies ; the same for favors, tied with ribbon to match. Marguerites and lily of the valley were also used with this combination for a young girl's luncheon.

For the luncheon of a yachting party, a skiff was suspended over the table, some five feet long. The hull was formed of water lilies, filled with adiantum. The favors were oars, made of foliage. A tank, made of ferns and greens, also decorated the center of one table, and was filled with pond lilies.

A green dinner : The center of the table was occupied by a mirror, partially concealed by the beautiful bank of ferns surrounding and overgrowing the supposed pool. A wax swan can be added when desired, and a canopy of smilax can hang from the chandelier over the table, from which a cupid or mermaid can be suspended. This has the appearance of diving in the liquid pool. (The edges of the glass should be so puttied that it will allow of a thin sheet of water on it.) Flat baskets of the same for the smaller table (for this purpose small two-inch pot plants of ferns are best, as they do not wilt so easily as the cut fronds), with a fairy lamp embedded inside, with the delicate fern fronds well up around it. White shades are the prettiest to use, but this depends on the taste ; pink shades could be used with a pink table cloth, with the foliage of green as described. Rex begonias work in beautifully in these fern effects, as also allamanda Schotti or Hendersonii, arranged loosely with lycopodiums and croton leaves. The favors were small crescents of Perle roses, with bow of satin of same shade. Cut glass and silver combine beautifully with lilies and pink roses. A vase of flowers, standing on a beveled mirror, with asparagus sprays for frame of mirror, is a pretty decoration.

Pea blossom luncheons are appropriate for young girls ; use sweet peas and mignonette, with pale pink cover ; clusters of the same for favors. Cherry, peach, apple and pear blossoms are beautiful for this purpose, as well as the double crab-apple and double peach and pear. Magnolias form a lovely spring arrangement.

A large flat basket of roses occupied the center of a table ; the roses were arranged in clusters, which were distributed before leaving the table to the guests ; favors of moss roses and violets.

A rich center piece consisted of a plant of adiantum Farleyense, with the drooping fronds well over the pot ; clusters of lily of the valley and Roman hyacinths rose up through the billowy fronds. This was set in an exquisite dish of silver, resting on a cream plush mat ; the favors were of lily of the valley with a frond of Farleyense fern. In strong contrast to this, yet beautiful, was an arrangement of grasses, field buttercups and daisies. You pay your money and you take your choice !

Sea foam dinner : On a plush mat of sea-foam tint, arrange adiantums of different kinds—for instance, adiantum bellum, cuneatum and Farleyense, with asparagus plumosa and tenuissimus. The *menu* card had a few fronds in crescent form encircling the card, tied with white satin ribbon.

Chrysanthemum dinner : A large flat basket, containing sections of bronze-colored, yellow and maroon chrysanthemums, with stevia compacta sprayed very lightly over the surface, finished with autumn leaves and croton foliage. (It is a mistake, I think, to arrange chrysanthemums with fern leaves, unless they are coarse, woodsy ferns.) Small Japanese fans of yellow and maroon chrysanthemums, tied with old gold ribbon, are pretty for favors.

Fish lying on a platter : An oval platter, formed of closely set carnations, on which lay a floral fish. The belly was of variegated vinca leaves, the back being formed of the plain green leaves of the same variety. A spray consisting of a half blown rose, two buds and their foliage looked like a part of the decoration of the platter.

CHRISTENING GIFTS.

A cradle of carnations, with a canopy of white, lined with pale pink balsams ; the "baby"—a choice wax doll—lay inside, kicking his pink toes up through the flowers. " Too sweet for anything " was the verdict expressed. A cover was made for this design formed of tiny squares of carnations, with lines of sweet alyssum ; three tiny pink rosebuds were placed in the center of this spread, while white begonias were used for fringe.

Baby's toilet basket, the pockets of which were filled with lily of the valley and rosebuds. Basket of moss rose buds, tied with white satin ribbon ; baby of wax lying in it, with cluster of forget-me-not at one side. Basket of blue satin filled with marguerites (in this case, the child's name was Daisy).

Little socks, filled with pea blossoms, begonias and other fine blossoms. Perambulators of gilt, with lining of pale blue satin, filled with white rosebuds.

Thus, we close with tributes to the first year of life, instead of its end, with the hope that all are looking forward to achievements to come, and not on those already past.

ADVERTISEMENTS.

(149)

Chrestensen's • •

Makart Prize Bouquets

Manufactured by

N. L. Chrestensen,

Erfurt, Germany.

THESE BOUQUETS are artistically made from materials gathered from all parts of the world, and form most beautiful and attractive ornaments for parlors, drawing rooms, etc. They are either round or flat in form, and are very handsome placed in a corner or other part of a room. They have been highly commended everywhere, and are offered with much confidence. A sample arrangement may be seen on page 103 of this book.

WE ARE THE LARGEST HANDLERS OF THESE GOODS IN THE WORLD.

Prices of Makart Bouquets:

Each

In Round Form, about 3 feet in diameter, including packing, $5 00

"   "   "   5   "   "   "   "   7 50

In Flat Form, from 1 to 5 feet high . . . . . . 75 cents to 6 00

Vases.

Also, a large assortment of beautiful vases, suitable for containing Makart Bouquets, at from 65 cents to $6 each.

MAKART CATALOGUES, with full particulars, will be sent free on application.

Address

N. L. CHRESTENSEN,
Erfurt, Germany.

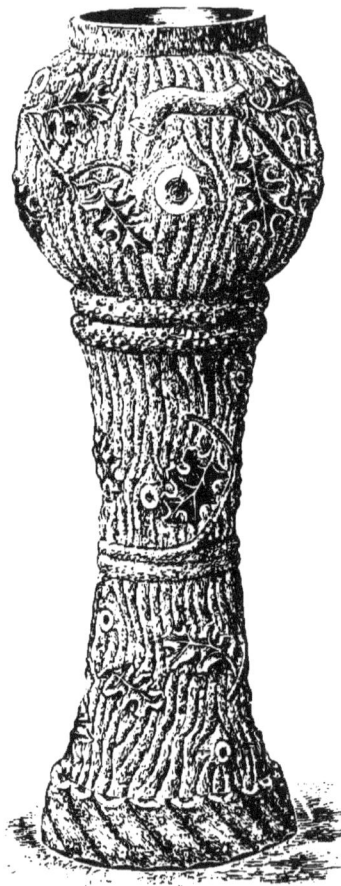

SIEBRECHT & WADLEY,

Rose Hill Nurseries,

NEW ROCHELLE, NEW YORK.

City Office: 409 Fifth Avenue, New York.

A SUPERB STOCK OF ALL

Decorative Plants

PALMS, ORCHIDS, ETC.

CUT ORCHIDS AND CUT LEAVES OF CYCAS REVOLUTA

Supplied at any time, at most reasonable rates. Correspond for prices and particulars, and remember we are headquarters for Orchids and fine Decorative Stock.

(154)

MONEY SAVING APPLIANCES

FOR FLORISTS.

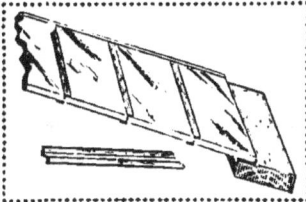

J. M. Gasser's
Patent Zinc Joints

FOR GLAZING GREENHOUSES WITHOUT LAPPING THE GLASS.

This method of glazing makes an air and water tight roof, saving fuel and glass, and enabling a more even temperature to be maintained. It also obviates the danger of breakage from frost, or of glass slipping out of place.

They are readily applied, inexpensive, and result in a large saving. Write for prices, giving size of glass you intend to use.

J. M. Gasser's
Patent Oil Burner

FOR BURNING CRUDE PETROLEUM.

This is a simple but automatic apparatus, and is thoroughly successful in operation. It is especially adapted for greenhouse heating, because it can be relied upon to make steam or heat water all night without attention. Where crude oil can be readily obtained, it is

cheaper than coal and better than natural gas, without any of the danger of the latter. It is most easily regulated, and when you wish to stop your fire, all expense ceases, with no handling of coal or ashes.

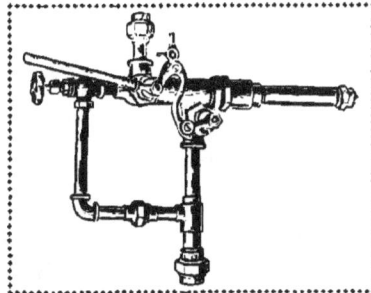

Hughes Improved
Duplex Pumps

Are especialty adapted for florists who wish to pump their own water. They are well made in every particular, and have a safety device which enables them to be operated without the slightest danger.

Reliance Safety
Water Column.

A safety device intended for use on steam boilers. Gives an alarm for both *high and low water automatically*. Just the the thing for florists who heat by steam. Write for circulars and prices to

J. M. GASSER, 101 Euclid Avenue, Cleveland, Ohio.

(155)

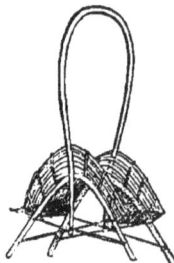

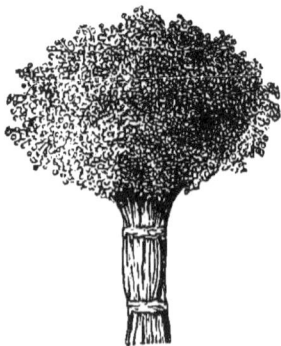

The Attention of Florists and Seedsmen

IS CALLED TO

SCRIBNER'S MAGAZINE

AS A

MEDIUM FOR ADVERTISING FLOWERS AND SEEDS.

The extended circulation of this Magazine, and the high character of its constituents, render it especially valuable, and it has been extensively used during the season by the leading Florists and Seedsmen of the country.

ADVERTISING RATES.

Per page, one time $150 00
" one-half page, one time 80 00
" one-fourth page, " 45 00
" Nonpareil line 1 00

☞Discounts for three insertions, 5 per cent. ; for six insertions, 10 per cent.; for twelve insertions, 20 per cent. Nonpareil lines run twelve to the inch.

The Magazine retails for 25 cents per number; subscriptions, $3.00 per year.

Any communication will receive prompt attention if addressed to

Magazine Department, Chas. Scribner's Sons,

NO. 743 BROADWAY, NEW YORK CITY.

(157)

(158)

ELLA GRANT CAMPBELL,
• Floral Artist •
275 Jennings Ave., Cleveland, Ohio.

DESIGNS OF FLOWERS made to order on short notice, and shipped to all parts of the United States within 600 miles of Cleveland. Fifteen to twenty per cent. commission allowed on all orders sent by florists at retail prices. Our facilities for packing are unexcelled. Price List sent on application. Try an order.

Baskets, Wire Designs, Stemming Materials, Cape Flowers and Other Florists' Supplies

Always on hand. We make a specialty of Designs made of Cape Flowers and Immortelles. Address

MRS. ELLA GRANT CAMPBELL,
276 Jennings Avenue, Cleveland, Ohio.

A. BLANC,

314 North Eleventh Street,

PHILADELPHIA, PA.

Engraver for Florists, Seedsmen and Nurserymen

HEADQUARTERS FOR

Horticultural Illustrations

IN GREAT VARIETY.

Printing, Binding,

THIS BOOK is a sample of the work done by J. HORACE MCFARLAND COMPANY, HARRISBURG, PA., specialists in printing for Nurserymen, Florists and Seedsmen. Combining a thorough practical knowledge of the requirements of horticultural printing with an excellent equipment in both machinery, material and cuts, the Mount Pleasant Printery is enabled to produce results unattainable in the best ordinary establishments. Correspondence is invited from those desiring good work, well illustrated and of assured accuracy.

Electrotyping.

INDEX.

FULL PAGE PLATES OF DESIGNS.

DESCRIPTIVE MATTER, ETC.

(162)

www.ingramcontent.com/pod-product-compliance
Lightning Source LLC
Chambersburg PA
CBHW020550270326
41927CB00006B/790